BLOWING THE WHISTLE

BLOWING THE WHISTLE

Toni Schumacher

Translated by Chris Morris

A STAR BOOK
published by
the Paperback Division of
W. H. Allen & Co. PLC

A Star Book
Published in 1988
by the Paperback Division of
W. H. Allen & Co. PLC
44 Hill Street, London W1X 8LB

First published in West Germany under the title
Anpfiff by Droemer Knaur 1987
This translation copyright © W. H. Allen, 1987
Photographs courtesy of Colorsport

Copyright © Droemersche Verlagsanstalt Th. Knaur Nachf Munich 1987

Printed in Great Britain by
Cox & Wyman Ltd, Reading

ISBN 0 352 32194 6

CONTENTS

1	The Final	1
2	From Harald to Toni	15
3	The Battiston Affair	33
4	The Monster of Seville	47
5	Rummenigge Alone Against the Mafia	63
6	Mexico	81
7	Sex and Dope	91
8	The Spectre of Injury	103
9	A Camel with the Heart of a Lion	113
10	The National Side	129
11	The Bundeslige: an Idle Bunch	141
12	Sport: a Multimillion-Dollar Business	157
13	The Adidas-Puma Wrangle	167
14	Football as a Spectator Sport	181
15	The Press	189
16	The Prospect of Early Retirement	203
17	The English Game	207

1

THE FINAL

IT'S ALWAYS the same.

For weeks on end, players and sports officials had been living together, more or less amicably. Training together. Eating together. Even sharing sleeping accommodation. Fits of hysterical laughter or angry outbursts, tension and clashes — such are the consequences of communal life when you put together nearly thirty adults whose dominant characteristics — not to say professional qualities — are pride and an ego the size of a furniture removal van.

And then all this was suddenly forgotten, swept aside. We all became as polite and timid and moderate as monks in a monastery. Team-mates all but started addressing each other as strangers. We *did* become strangers to each other. No, it was worse that that: we became strangers to ourselves.

Outside the hotel, in Mexico, just as were about to get on the coach, Hermann Neuberger, Egidius Braun and all the other West German team officials and supervisors came to see us off, and to wish us luck.

There was a strange apprehension in their eyes as they focused on some distant point over our shoulders. There was awkwardness and reserve. The very few words spoken seemed incongruous and obtrusive. The fear of failure was invisible and unspoken. Intense, indescribable feelings. Huge responsibilities.

I'm the goalkeeper in the West German squad. I've played in two European championships. This is my second World Cup tournament. This time I want to be world champion. No messing about. Each match is a challenge. And today more so than ever. I'm trembling with emotion, with excitement. The other players are quiet. With good reason. Only in silence is there any stature; all else is pathetic.

I want to become world champion.

For four years I've wrestled with the lazy swine that I am deep down inside, I've struggled relentlessly to conquer my own mediocrity. I've trained with iron discipline, every hour, every day. Will these sacrifices soon be rewarded?

Franz Beckenbauer, world champion in 1974, a 'big brother' to us and our coach, moves about with the stiffness of a Prussian general. His eyes gleam with an energy that he seems to want to transmit to us. I can understand the tension and nervousness this once inspired player must be feeling. Now his job condemns him to have no control over winning or losing, except mentally. Those agile legs of his are of no help or use to him now.

'Schumacher lives inside his body as though it were a prison,' he once said of me. But today he's in the same position. And perhaps more so than I am.

Matthäus has a sombre determined look in his eye. He knows what's expected of him. He has an overwhelming responsibility in this game. One that doesn't seem to worry him too much. He is to be Maradona's marker and keep the Argentinian striker out of the game. This is his assignment.

The final against Argentina must be played as though it were a ten-a-side match. With the Matthäus–Maradona duel a separate issue. Our strategy is simple, not to say stupid. To neutralize Maradona, the football genius. As for the rest, we're relying on the German team's fighting spirit!

I feel sorry for Rummenigge, our own football genius. I admire him enormously, despite the stupid things he's said about me, and about the so-called 'Cologne Mafia', of which I'm supposed to be the Godfather and which supposedly hounds him and persecutes him. Poor martyr!

Today his face looks as fresh and pink as a little marzipan pig. But either side of his nose is deeply lined. He claims to be in great shape. But he's worked like an animal to reach his form. I take my hat off to him! What's going on in his mind right this minute? Will his brain, his intelligence hamper his creativity, his goal-scoring instinct? Will his reflexes be curbed, inhibited or, worse still, destroyed?

I know what the after-effects of an injury are like. I know that feeling of hesitation that creeps up on you at the decisive moment. Will those injured muscles and ligaments stand up to the impact? Will they tear? These questions are always at the back of your mind. So you need a truly iron will to do violence to your own body, the tool you work with. Pushing back the barriers of pain is an eternal struggle. Suppressing the pain to the extreme limit, to the point where you can't take it any more. For me, pain is just an illusion. Does Karl-Heinz Rummenigge know this too? I hope so. For his sake and for ours.

* * *

We're on the coach en route to the Mexico Stadium. I'm sitting on the back seat, on the right. This is where I invariably sit. Mexico's grubby light penetrates the curtain that I've drawn across the window.

Heat and chaos.

The air in this town is stifling, despite the air-conditioning. We're late, and to cap it all we're trapped in one of Mexico's legendary traffic jams.

The headphones of my Walkman are pressing on my ears. I'm immersed in the music of Peter Maffray, my favourite German rock singer. His music shields me from the town, from this thousand-eyed crowd that I sense rather than see through the windows of the coach. The words of the song fit this situation exactly: 'I'm strong only with a gut anger . . . I'm prepared to be torn apart for my friends . . . I gladly give you your revenge and I'm strong only with a gut love and anger.'

Mexico Stadium. Bright colours. Flags. Doves of peace everywhere. The crowd roaring and shouting. Bread and circuses.

Am I also a gladiator? Or one of the wild beasts? I don't like anybody inside this stadium. But I don't feel any gut hatred or anger. What revenge is that guy Maffray talking about, I wonder? I simply want to become world champion and my opponents are not necessarily my enemies. I've played a clean game so far in this World Cup. Just a couple of days ago I massaged the Mexican Hugo Sanchez's legs – he was suffering from cramp and crying out in pain. And I consoled him, as well as Negrete, off the field, after Mexico's defeat. It wasn't just an act, or put on for show. Contrary to what some cynics have suggested, there was no element of calculation in what I did; it was quite spontaneous.

Training and warm-up session for the German team.

The assistant coach, Horst Köppel, puts me through my paces. I'm sweating, already my throat is dry. And this rock-hard, hostile pitch, like dried shit.

I watch Karl-Heinz Förster. He exudes power and the kind of robustness that you know you can always rely on. The sight of his calmness, of his solid presence, does me good. I could hug him just for being there.

The sun is now directly over the stadium. It's beating down on our heads. There isn't an inch of shade anywhere. Which is very good for the picture on the screen, they say. The Mexicans are relaying these matches to TV stations all over the world. One and a half billion viewers . . . It's enough to send shivers up your spine. Best not to think about it. Anyway, thinking is poisonous. It's a poison that paralyses you.

National anthems.

'You're the best goalkeeper in the world. You're going to stop every ball. You're a beast of prey, Harald Schumacher.'

This is what I focus my mind on during endless, countless concentration exercises. It's a trick of mine for sharpening my reflexes. It has always worked till now. This is what I tell myself while the national anthem of our Argentinian opponents is playing. Then I close my eyes.

I'm sure lots of people think that 'Toni', being a chauvinist, has fallen into some kind of patriotic trance. Far from it! I'm simply letting myself escape temporarily into another world: a sandy beach stretching away for ever . . . a light breeze that makes the palm trees wave like fans . . . I'm swimming in a deep-blue lagoon somewhere in the Pacific . . .

Returning from an inward voyage of this kind, I feel better. My concentration is perfect. I have only one thought in mind: 'You're the best goalkeeper. No ball can get past you. You're a tiger: the ball is your prey.'

This is the secret of my ability to concentrate 150 percent. To be ready to stop every shot at goal.

So before the kick-off against Argentina, I went through the exercise again. I told myself: 'This is your big day. The game of your life. You're at the peak of your form. You stopped a penalty in the match against Mexico. And you played like a god against France.'

I felt as though I had wings. I was superconfident.

The final begins. A glance to right and left. No sign of any prey. Twenty long minutes go by. Too long. Not a single shot at goal.

I'm hungry for the ball, and it's a hunger that increases with every minute that passes. But nothing . . . Not a thing in sight . . .

Then comes that fatal free kick, a cross that will lead to the first goal. An Argentinian lines up the ball. My prey! It comes flying in my direction. I move out towards it, determined to catch it.

'This one's yours! You're going to get this one!'

I rush forward. From the moment I start moving I know that I'm not going to catch anything. Every hundredth of a second seems like an eternity. I go sailing across the penalty area like Lohengrin sailing past his swan. My last hope: 'Will a German player manage to head the ball away?'

But it wasn't to be. An Argentine head gets there first and tips the ball into the back of the net. I watch this catastrophe, dumbfounded. But inwardly I'm silently shouting.

Can it be that creativity suffers from too much concentration? I made no excuses. There was no point in dwelling on it.

'I gladly give you your revenge,' Maffray sang in my Walkman headphones.

Will there be any revenge for me? I'm sweating. I'm

going to lose another three kilos again in this match. Despite the torrid heat, I feel cold. I'd promised myself I was going to prove that I was the best keeper in the world, that I wasn't going to make any mistakes: 'And this is how you start the final! So much for wanting to play like a god!'

I have no choice now: for the remaining seventy-five minutes I have to play a perfect game! Like a faultless machine. And make everyone forget how I leapt like a damned nanny-goat into the void. What a fool I made of myself! What about that wild beast I'm supposed to be?

A goalkeeper never scores a goal. And he can't correct his mistakes. He can only envy the striker who with a single shot that finds the mark can wipe out a hundred balls that he's sent sky-high. For a keeper, it's all or nothing. Success or failure. He's either a king or a nobody.

I really hate myself. Now I've got that gut anger.

The 'prey' is still bouncing around. A long way off. No threat. And then suddenly dangerous. It's brought under control and kicked about by Germans and Argentinians. Matthäus is still marking Maradona closely, but all the same the field is swarming with Argentinians.

One of them breaks away. Valdano. He's got the ball. I run forward and try to draw him. I give him an opening as I move towards him. He goes the other way. The prey grazes past my knee, out of reach, and carries on to the back of the net.

'Stay on the line,' shout Förster and Magath.

Rummenigge manages to score off a corner taken by Brehme. 1–2. Jubilation. A little later, comes an unhoped-for equaliser. 2–2. We go wild.

The Germans are always on the offensive. Much too often. We're taking too many risks.

'Stay on the line,' my team-mates told me.

Five minutes before the end of the game, an Argentinian

breaks away with the ball and comes hurtling towards me.
I have to come off the line. But I hesitate. This time I get
there too late. And the penalty for misjudging it is I let
another goal through.

The whistle goes and it's the end of the match.

There's no extra time. No penalties I could have saved –
penalties that I would have to have saved to redeem my
mistakes.

'A good goalkeeper is a player who's in a position, at
several points during a game, to save his side. By his
individual efforts, by going beyond his capability in a
voluntary act.' So said Jean-Paul Sartre. And he was
right.

But this time I haven't saved anything. I didn't go
beyond my capabilities.

Had I become a bad goalkeeper?

Dejection – no, depression is the word to describe the
feeling that washes over you from head to foot when
you've lost a final. You think you're going to die.

The winning side are elated. They leap around, their
tiredness and exhaustion forgotten. The losers feel
thrashed, beat, bone tired. Our plucky midfield player
Briegel has tears in his eyes. Rummenigge is deathly pale.
The disappointment in the German side is tremendous.
The losers are alone in the midst of this crowd shouting
with joy. And every one of the eleven defeated players is
alone with himself. The eleventh man, the keeper, the
outsider in the game, is on his own yet again.

Only victory creates a sense of union within a side.

I feel I'm to blame. A missed ball is an opportunity lost
for ever.

Frustration. Empty hands. A wind inside my head.

Half an hour after the final a journalist from RTL
interviews me:

'What happened, Toni?'

My reply was as simple as it was crude:

'I played like an arsehole! If I'd been as good as I was against France and Mexico, we'd be world champions this evening. That's all there is to it.'

I would have given anything to be world champion. Well, not anything . . . Not my children. Not my parents either. Nor my wife, Marlies, nor Rüdiger Schmitz, my friend and personal manager. But otherwise, I'd have given anything. Including my health.

I would have been prepared never to play football again after this final if I could have become world champion. The best in the world!

I've missed my chance. I know that for me there isn't going to be a next time. Football isn't like ice-hockey, where there's a world championship every year. For us footballers, four years is a long time. In Spain, and in Mexico, the German team has had to be content with second place. And by the time the next World Cup comes round, I'll be thirty-six.

I hate letting goals in! But what's the use of moaning on about it? Football without any goals would be like capitalism without bankruptcies, or Christianity without Hell.

Those are the rules of the game, and they apply as much to the only man on the field who has the right to handle the ball as they do to anybody else.

'Show me a man who's happy coming second,' Hennes Weisweiler, one of my coaches at Cologne, is in the habit of saying, 'and I'll show you the eternal loser.'

He was right, old 'Don Hennes'.

The only thing to do is get away. Make for the cloak-rooms underneath the stadium. Everyone wants to feast their eyes on the winners and salute them. But only the winners. The losers have to disappear from the field as quickly as possible, and sink into anonymity.

In the little white bag that contains my spare gloves and peaked cap, I've packed a few other things: talismans from Greece and Turkey, presents from fans. Lucky charms: a knitted doll, a small pig . . . I'm never without them. Partly because I think they're cute, partly because I'm superstitious.

The most important thing is a photograph of my son Oliver. I was there when he was born. It was wonderful. But that day I felt helpless, useless . . . My wife, Marlies, held my hand.

I couldn't help her. I felt so vulnerable. To be there, with your wife, and not to be able to do anything!

After that defeat in Mexico I looked at Oliver's photo. And I said to myself: 'Look, Toni, at least you've got healthy kids.' That suddenly made me feel better and gave me new strength. I was ready to face the world again, and the press and officials.

I know that I deserve my enemies. But I'm not going to let this get me down.

Since the 'foul' I committed on Battiston in Spain, in 1982, I'm perfectly well aware that people have a negative view of me. There are plenty who would like to topple Schumacher from his pedestal. A bit like Muhammad Ali, in his day. He was another big-mouth, but what class!

'People can't stand a big-mouth but they always listen to him,' the black American boxer used to say.

And everyone hopes and wishes that he'll lose one day, at least once. Before Mexico, people regarded me as a kind of monster. A block of marble standing in front of the net. A guy with no human feelings whatsoever, and only one concern: not to let any goals in!

The perfect German machine, as it were.

And then I go and make a terrible mistake, the kind of mistake only a thoroughly ordinary human being could make. My critics were completely thrown by this, like dancers who start a fox-trot on the wrong foot. I was inundated with messages of sympathy. People felt sorry for me; even the press.

I had finally matured. I had acquired a human aspect. All this is a bit simplistic – although kindly meant, I admit. In fact, I had always been human. But crazier than most, more obsessed too by my responsibility in goal. For years I had been classified as some kind of wild animal, and given a place in humanity's chamber of horrors. Because I was German, people thought I was made of the same metal as the torturers at Auschwitz. And now people were beginning to see me in a more favourable light.

I was delighted by this wave of sympathy. A real balm to my injured pride. But nice though this new sympathy was, I couldn't forget that it was just the tide turning after years of mistrust and hostility towards me. I'd never been a monster. Just an ordinary guy who wanted to be successful.

Uli Stein, the Hamburg goalkeeper and for a long time the number two keeper for the German side, said one day that I would walk over dead bodies to succeed. True! But only my own, in order to win. That might seem a bit extreme, but that's the way I am. And people have to take me as I am or not at all.

There are no half-measures for a goalkeeper. He can't say: 'In today's training session I'm going to soft-pedal it, perform at half-cock.' Any keeper who thinks like this will let goal after goal get past him in the next match. Let me say it again; if a centre-forward scores in the last minute of a match, he's king. A keeper makes a mistake at the same crucial moment, and he lets a goal in, he's everybody's

fool. Worse: a pariah. No one will stand up for him. If you
have two friends in life, you're doing well . . .

To be professional means selling yourself body and soul
to the club you sign up with. When I signed up with FC
Cologne I told them: 'Here I am, my body, my health, my
life, my soul. I'm all yours.'

On the other hand, I'm well paid.

But there's a limit to everything. For instance, no way am
I going to let myself be degraded and become a passive tool
of club managers or ambitious politicians.

Mexico. On the podium in the stadium.

Chancellor Helmut Kohl came to Mexico in the hope of
being able to bask in the glow of our victory. But as it turned
out he was almost more disappointed than we were, if that's
possible. The Chancellor congratulated us, but he was just
going through the motions; his smile was fixed, like a rictus.

In a scene worthy of a comic opera, he seized Beckenbauer by the shoulder, and made him turn to face the
photographers so that they could get a picture of him
standing next to our coach. Footballers turned into politicians' puppets and exploited to demonstrate 'national
unity'. When sport joins hands with politics, naïvety meets
calculation.

The Sheraton Hotel. I can't bear to stay to the end of the
gala dinner. Champagne has a bitter taste when you've
come second in the World Cup.

To be alone – that's all I want. Back in my room, I break
into a cold sweat. We've lost a battle. Is football a substitute
for warfare? No, not really, When you win, you win everything. When you lose, you're still alive.

Snatches of experience. Scenes of a defeat. The feelings of
a national goalkeeper. I know that I'm both the judge and
the accused. Am I in danger of being too hard or too soft on
myself?

Who am I really? A keeper capable of putting on a dazzling display, but who occasionally risks getting on the wrong side of his employers? Am I a good husband at home, a cold-as-ice professional on the field? A sensitive soul beneath a rough exterior, as Pisceans are supposed to be? Am I the beast the press described, after my foul on Battiston in 1982? Or the victim of action replay, showing every move, every false step, every foul over and over again until hatred has been whipped up?

People say writing is a form of confession, an exploration of the self. For me, it is above all a way of escaping my isolation. It's not intended to be a navel-gazing exercise. And still less some kind of justification of myself and my behaviour. What I aim to do is to act as a prism and cast light on my world, the world of football, in Germany and on the international stage.

By describing the rollercoaster ride that my career has been, I would like to let you have an exclusive behind-the-scenes look at my sport. It's going to be an occasionally bumpy ride. I'm going to criticize the players as much as the coaches, managers and other club officials, at league and national level. Not an indiscriminate demolition job. I don't want to do down any institution, or foul any player or manager. I simply want to stimulate some thinking about the crises, the opportunities and the challenges that face the sport that is my life.

2

FROM HARALD TO TONI

MY FAVOURITE film is *Rocky*, with Sylvester Stallone. Rocky, the slum kid who's determined to be a winner. He wants to beat his opponent, of course, but he also wants to beat poverty and fate.

'That's you,' I said to myself, 'you're the Rocky of the football world. A guy who wants to climb out of the gutter.'

My own slum childhood was spent in Düren, near Cologne, a town that was badly bombed during the Second World War. As kids, we liked to play in the ruins. We used to live on a housing estate. Our neighbours were poor. I used to watch the decline of whole families: most of the fathers were alcoholics; most of the mothers slovenly shrews.

Of course there were good people as well. But there was poverty everywhere, wherever you looked. We never ate meat at home. Our diet consisted mainly of potatoes, and more potatoes. And occasionally a cabbage leaf as a special treat. Not a very varied diet. But others were worse off.

My sister and I shared a tiny room, not much bigger than a cupboard. Ever since living in such cramped conditions,

I've been an incurable claustrophobic. There's nothing I can do about it.

It's the same on the pitch; I can't stay on the line. It's my need for open space that makes me venture out of my area as often as I can.

My father was a construction worker. He used to leave for work every morning at seven o'clock. He would come home in the evening completely shattered, locked in silence. In winter, he would stretch his tired legs out in front of the only stove in the house. For a long time, what the word 'father' meant to me was a pair of legs in front of the fire. He didn't drink, thank God.

My father was a simple, quiet, honest man. And he's the same today. Without him, without the example of his calmness and decency, I might perhaps have got into bad ways. Many of the friends I had then have followed the bad example of their drunken fathers.

My mother too had a great influence on me. I used to watch her sew for other people, day in, day out. She was always telling me: 'Poverty's nothing to be ashamed of, son. The important thing is to be honest and hard-working. And not to do anything shameful.'

As well as a sandpit for toddlers in the playground near where we lived, there was also plenty of room to play football. Football became a form of release for me, a way of enjoying myself and escaping the family's hardships. I played as a forward – a position I could really shine in.

'That boy is a fighter,' people used to say about me. 'He'll make his way.'

Those who are by nature fighters live more dangerously than other people, even as children.

'You run too much, Harald,' my coach used to say. 'You're going to run yourself into the ground. You must learn to use your energy and strength better.'

My mother would echo that: 'It's true, Harald comes home completely exhausted, covered in sweat. He can't hold himself back. He's always got this compulsion to do everything at full throttle. And he isn't really all that robust.'

Both my coach and my mother used to worry about my health. Until the day my mother put her foot down.

'That's enough,' she said. 'It's time you moved to a position that doesn't involve so much excitement and running about. Go and play goalkeeper. That'll suit you much better.'

That's how I became a goalkeeper, on my mother's orders. Because it was a less exciting position to play in. I was eleven at the time.

But even in goal, I still had the same temperament and the same determination to go all the way. Just like Rocky!

I had a very clear view of my situation: I was poor. Getting a school-leaving certificate was out of the question, let alone going on to higher education. But I was going to show all those guys who *were* able to study what *I* was capable of!

I wasn't envious. But I couldn't understand why some people inherited a place in the sun at birth, while others were condemned to living under an eternal raincloud.

Those who are lucky enough to benefit from their parents' wealth aren't to blame. And it's stupid to envy them. You have to take a broader view.

I've had to fight hard for everything, because I wasn't particularly talented. But the fighters do better in the end than those who've had exceptional talent bestowed upon them by Nature. Looking back, I'm totally convinced of this.

A handicap overcome can turn into a positive advantage, a challenge that helps you conquer the highest

peaks. Barbra Streisand eventually made it, despite the
squint in her eyes, and so did Clark Gable, even though he
had such a bad stammer it was pitiful.

An iron will and hard work are the keys to success. In
my case, it was will power that was the most important. In
the contest between keeper and striker, I performed well
from the start. I wasn't afraid of injury, I didn't stop to
consider the danger. I was only interested in winning, in
being the best!

When I was fifteen, I was already training four times a
week. Twice with the juniors, twice with the first team. I
lived like a monk. I had no time for girls. I never dreamed
of owning a motorbike, and I only saw discotheques from
the outside. I lived only for football, nothing else.

My idols were the star goalkeepers of the 60s: Toni
Tureck and Fritz Heckenrath.

Every Sunday, my own performance on the field gave
me an opportunity to win respect and admiration. I would
tank up with enough pride to last for the rest of the week
and forget the area where I lived, the hardship, the
poverty.

'Did you see how Harald played again,' people would
whisper.

'That's Helga and Manfred's son. That boy has a
future.'

This was music to my ears.

Social advancement through football? That's how it
was for me. I could see the parallel between my position
and that of other social outsiders. It's no accident that the
majority of Olympic jumpers and sprinters are black. Like
them, I wanted recognition. Glory. There are days when I
can't understand why all blacks aren't world champions
of one kind or another.

At the beginning of the 80s, we had a young black

player at FC Cologne, Toni Baffoe. He was eighteen and
wanted to become a professional footballer. His performance was erratic. He was too easily discouraged and began
to doubt his capabilities. His attitude drove me mad.

'If I were black,' I told him, 'which is the reason why a
lot of people treat you like shit – if I were like you, at the
bottom of the ladder, the colour of my skin would be
enough to drive me to become the best player in the world.
Don't let anything stop you. Show them what you can do.'

Unfortunately Baffoe didn't have my will power, and he
didn't share the strong aversion I have to all forms of
humiliation.

When I was sixteen, the dance class I had been
attending celebrated the end of the course with a party. I
had successfully managed to overcome my shyness and
master the tango. The girls were pretty and I made sure
even my fingernails were clean. Over the past months, I
had enjoyed myself with classmates of my own age; we
drank Coca Colas together, having fun and squabbling
amongst ourselves.

And now the long-awaited party was to take place –
giving rise to a drama, as it turned out, over what I was to
wear. The suit I had worn to make my First Communion
hadn't fitted me for a long time. I didn't have any cousins
my age from whom I could have borrowed one. There was
just my father's dark-blue suit. . .

'No way will I wear that,' I told my mother. 'Dad's suit
will look like a saddle on a pig on me. You'll have to buy
me one!'

'And where's the money to pay for it coming from? Just
who do you think you are? You're suffering delusions of
grandeur.'

Seething with anger, I put on my father's suit, which
was specially ironed for the occasion, but I had to wear

braces because the trousers were too big for me. Whilst all
my friends were properly dressed for the party, I felt like a
country bumpkin. I've rarely felt as unhappy as I did that
evening. I thought of myself as a black with a white
skin . . .

I put my heart and soul into training, having set myself a
number of targets to reach on my way to the summit. First
of all, Düren. Then a regional team. Then one of the
Bundeslige clubs, and finally the National Youth Team.
It all went according to plan until the end of the 60s. The
coach of the German Youth Team was then Herbert
Widmayer. He had seen me play in several matches. But
the decisive moment came after a trial match for a place in
the team. At the end of the game there was a series of
penalties. I stopped three out of five. After that, my name
was on everyone's lips.

'Schumacher, from Düren. Keep an eye on that boy, he
looks promising.'

The talent scouts from the regional and national clubs
had been tipped off. They were watching me. The offer of
a place in the Youth Team came just a few weeks later. I
then discovered that most of the players in the German
Youth Team were already signed up with clubs in the
Bundeslige. Jupp Rohring, the coach for FC Cologne's
youth team, suggested I make a similar arrangement with
them.

I was sixteen, and very flattered.

But reluctantly, I had to refuse this offer.

'You need a trade,' my mother decided. 'Football can
come later, but first you're going to learn something
useful.'

No sooner said than done. I became a boilermaker, a
tough job. I got my certificate of apprenticeship and a

short while afterwards Rohring came knocking on my door again. This time, my mother agreed.

This marked a new beginning in my life.

Football. Nothing but football. My head was full of it, and I did nothing else. Every day of the week. Magic!

I turned professional, but there wasn't the same kind of pressure to perform well that I have today. There wasn't the same harassment by the press. Or the rivalry there is today. And the stress and obsession with being number one, and staying there.

For the first time in my life, I was earning money. A lot of money. One thousand, two hundred marks a month, at the age of eighteen. In my final year's apprenticeship I was only getting 320 marks a month. Now, I had an annual bonus of 30,000 DM. A total income of 45,000. I thought it was great. My father could never have scraped together so much money. Even working day and night.

Once in the National Youth Team, I quickly distinguished myself. I was a bit of star – or rather, starlet.

'That boy Schumacher is terrific!' I heard people say.

Actually, it quickly became apparent that I still had a few weak points – and I had to work extremely hard on them. For a while, I thought I was already one of the Greats. In fact, I was still a nobody.

Amateur and professional football have as much in common as a strawberry icecream and a skyscraper. The difference is enormous. Just as enormous as the challenge facing me. At that time the number one goalkeeper at Cologne was Gerhard Weltz. He was crazy, just like Rocky. He used to train like a man possessed.

'Schumacher,' I said to myself rather precociously, 'the position as keeper in the National Youth Team is yours for the taking.'

I very quickly realised that it wasn't as simple as that.

These professional strikers attacked like real demons. As quick as lightning. Their shots at goal were ultrapowerful, and always found the corners of my net. These balls, which Weltz frequently stopped, were still out of my reach.

A difficult period followed. I was allowed to play in unimportant matches. Not a single Bundeslige game, or Cup match. I was vegetating. I'd play the odd half-game here, a friendly match there. Not the slightest chance of a breakthrough.

Despite the punishing training programme, nothing. I was kicking my heels. Until the day Weltz suffered a groin and head injury.

A lucky break? My lucky break? You must be joking! I was allowed to share the number one shirt with Topalovic, a Yugoslav. FC Cologne chose to field two averagely good keepers rather than treat itself to one excellent keeper. How far away the time of my naïve hopes seemed then, the time when I'd had illusions as a member of the National Youth Team.

The first hour's training with Rolf Herings, the man who coached the goalkeepers at FC Cologne, was my hour of reckoning. The balls whistled past my ears. I was unable to stop a single one.

Years later, Rolf told me: 'That day, after our session together, your morale was rock bottom. All the cockiness was gone. You couldn't take the slighest criticism. You went leaping about for balls like a squirrel, before falling flat on your stomach like an overripe plum falling off a tree. But you wanted to learn and do better. That was what most impressed me about you. The way you kept the bit between your teeth, even though you were completely exhausted, after hours of training. You were always prepared to give it everything you had, and more. You always used to say: "It's better than working eight hours a day as a boilermaker." That made a deep impression on me.'

A house-warming party at Mechernich, not far from Cologne. It was Heinz Flohe, a star of FC Cologne who also played for West Germany, throwing the party. He had just had a house built. A lovely big place, which cost him a fortune. The architect was none other than Rüdiger Schmitz, who was also Flohe's personal manager. Open-mouthed with admiration, I dreamt of a career to match Flohe's.

'Do you think Schmitz might take an interest in me?' I asked self-consciously.

'Of course!' he replied. 'You need a manager to bring some discipline to your game and your life.'

Schmitz was thirty-one; I was nineteen, shy, and no big-mouth – not any more. Just an ordinary young kid from the provinces. Right from the start I felt I could trust Rüdiger Schmitz. And he liked me, but that didn't stop him criticizing my keen attachment to my mother.

'Harald, you ought to distance yourself a bit from your background, from Düren and from your childhood,' he advised me, 'otherwise you'll never make the break-through.'

He knew how much I loved my mother and it didn't bother him at all – in principle. What did bother him was that whenever I had the slightest doubt about anything, or about myself, I would always, without fail, turn to her. I could rely on my mother to support and bolster me, without reservation.

Rüdiger would get annoyed.

'It's a real poison this mania of yours for always seeking consolation from your mother. Especially when you've done the stupidest things. There's no place for any Mummy's-boys in professional football.'

I didn't really know what to say. I was very upset.

'Spontaneity, ambition, even brutality are the qualities required of you. Start by cutting your umbilical cord, otherwise you'll keep getting your feet tangled up in it.'

At first, I turned to Rüdiger for help instead of the parental home, but as time went by he left me to deal with my problems by myself. In this way, he encouraged me, kindly but firmly, to come to terms with myself, to take responsibility for myself. It was difficult; a path paved with humiliations. I felt constantly under pressure and often out of my depth.

My performance in goal from 1973 to '77 earned me the inglorious nickname of 'the Fidget'. Weisweiler, who became my coach in 1976, never criticized me to my face. He simply ignored me. The better to ridicule me when I wasn't there. Unfortunately, Hennes Weisweiler is now dead. May he rest in peace. He was an excellent coach, but a very poor psychologist. Instead of offering constructive criticism, he could come out with a torrent of sarcasm and mockery that was very upsetting. One fine day he decided to 'let me go' to another club. I was deeply shocked, hurt and humiliated.

'Get rid of Schumacher,' he told the club directors, so I heard.

This episode was what finally made me decide to leave FC Cologne. As it was, I was only occasionally getting a place in the team. I was ready to throw in the towel.

At that time Rüdiger Schmitz had a house on the Eifel, just on the edge of a forest. We used to walk for hours there.

'It calms you down,' Rüdiger used to say with a smile. 'The fresh air clears the smoke from a hothead's brain.'

But after we'd walked a few paces, he stopped and said in a suddenly serious voice: 'You're still a raw talent.' (His

voice sounded almost solemn.) 'You're like an uncut dia-
mond. How long will it need polishing before it reaches
perfection? I don't know. I only know that if you knuckle
down and work really hard to get rid of all your flaws, all
your rough edges, one day you'll succeed in allowing the
precious quality of your talent to shine through.'

These words marked the beginning of a new period for
me. Rüdiger insisted on very strict discipline. When he
said: 'Come at six o'clock', that meant six o'clock precisely. Not a minute sooner or later.

'Just concentrate on what your coach tells you and on
your team-mates' game,' he never tired of saying. 'No
other distractions for the time being.'

Schumacher, who'd previously had a reputation for
being one of the lads, became more serious, more
thoughtful. But the image of him as 'the Fidget' still stuck
in people's minds. The whole of Cologne was laughing
about Topalovic and me. We were the two 'cases' in the
team, always the subject of discussion among the directors, and a cause of concern to the club doctor. Slowly but
surely, I became a real bag of nerves.

'You want to be too good. You're excessively keen,' the
team doctor, Dr Bonnekoh, explained to me. 'Don't get so
worked up. Try to keep things in perspective, and keep
your cool. Why don't you try to learn to control yourself –
do some relaxation exercises, for instance.'

What next! My reaction was pigheaded.

'No way! In any case, I don't believe in this kind of
nonsense – horoscopes and the like.'

'Try it anyway. It can't hurt you. It's completely
harmless.'

I allowed myself to be persuaded by this excellent
reasoning and meekly made an appointment to see Dr
Schreckling, a very pleasant woman doctor.

'Think of something nice,' she began by telling me.
'Holidays, the beach, the sea, the sun, your family. Your
limbs are getting heavy, very heavy. The sun's shining, it's
warm. You're concentrating. You're playing. You want to
stop every ball, you want to devour them all. Like a tiger
lying in wait for its prey. Letting it approach and then
leaping on it like a flash of lightning . . .'

At first I spent about half an hour a day on these
exercises. Then I did six one-hour sessions a week to really
master the technique. I've used it regularly ever since, in
training and before every important match.

Concentration, relaxation. A thousand times over. Real
greatness lies in self-control. And that goes for the 1986
World Cup in that hellish dustbowl Monterrey . . . before
the penalty shootout against Mexico.

Franz Beckenbauer has described how he saw me then:

'Toni was sitting on the pitch. He was holding his head in
his hands. I knew that the game had completely drained
him. Even though he spends most of the time not moving, he
always loses at least five or six pints of sweat. He concen-
trates so hard he sometimes gets cramp. I went over to him.
No one can have any idea how tense Toni was. I certainly
couldn't imagine it. As a player, I was never faced with such
enormous rsponsibility. If you make a mistake and let the
penalty in, the whole team is out. Everyone's hopes rest on
your shoulders. I was standing beside him. He seemed to be
elsewhere. "What is it, Toni?" He didn't hear me. I said
again: "What's wrong?" Still no response. And then
suddenly, as though he had finally woken up, he said:
"Don't worry, Franz! Why should there be anything
wrong?" And he began to yawn. I honestly had the impression that I'd woken Schumacher from a deep sleep.'

Franz was right. I was elsewhere. I had withdrawn in
order to regenerate after the match.

Don't act on any premature reflexes. Wait . . .

In the minutes that followed I managed to stop two penalties.

Penalties are torture. You have to control your reflexes, and dive in only at the last hundredth of a second. Your body open and receptive to every sensation and stimulation, your head empty of thought. When it comes to the penalty kick, the keeper is to the other players what the madman is to normal people. He acts as a lightning conductor, just as the madman does. He's like a magnet that has to attract the ball as it whistles through the air onto his body.

It's thanks to Dr Schreckling that I can channel my energies to stop penalties.

To return to 1977, at that time the club manager was called Karl-Heinz Thielen – he resigned as Vice-President of FC Cologne in October 1986. He was not convinced of the effectiveness of my relaxation exercises. One fine day, with five games to play before the end of the championship, in his usual fashion he laid it on the line for me in no uncertain terms.

'Watch out, Toni, we're looking for a new keeper. To be blunt, we want to get rid of you. It's pointless carrying on like this. Weisweiler doesn't want to work with you any more.'

All that training, all that concentration, all that effort for nothing? And yet I was making fewer mistakes. The percentage of errors in my play had dropped from 30 to 27 percent.

My only hope was to make no mistakes at all in the remaining five matches. And if possible extend this error-free play until the German Cup Final. Although I was resigned to leaving Cologne, I decided to give of my best, if only to put myself in a better bargaining position when it came to changing clubs. There was already talk of Norbert Nigbur being my replacement. I felt a sense of frustration. Annoyance. Was I not going to be allowed a chance to show them what I was capable of? Topalovic, who was more often selected than me, was playing in all the championship matches. While I sat and waited on the touchline. In superfit condition! I finally got my break when we had to play a match in Berlin. Topalovic, who was terrified of flying, didn't want to go. I flew in his place . . . and managed to put on an amazing display. Not a single mistake. A scintillating performance. A one-all draw, thanks to me. I had become the number one star of Cologne. At last!

1977. Hanover. The final against Berlin. Norbert Nigbur, my potential successor, was at the other end of the pitch in goal for Hertha Berlin. I knew that my rival had already started negotiations with FC Cologne. That he would sign up with my club was virtually a foregone conclusion.

We won 1–0. An angry Nigbur had a go at the referee and accused him of having being bought by Cologne. After that, there was no question in the minds of the Cologne directors of Nigbur joining the club.

Two days later we were flying to Japan for a series of friendly matches. During the flight, Weisweiler, who only had time for good players, came and sat down beside me.

'Listen, Toni,' he growled, 'I'm not going to make any speeches, but there's one thing you should know: as far as I'm concerned, you're number one.'

A great wave of happiness. I felt as though I was walking on air again. But as Rüdiger Schmitz remarked drily, after I had taken a well-earned holiday: 'You'll never be the greatest, the best, unless you continue to put in at least 20 percent more training than anyone else.

Because the real fight begins when you're really knocked out. To feel KO and be able to say OK – that's the key to success.'

I'd already achieved a great deal. Little Harald from Düren had become the great Toni. Toni, short for Anton, my second name. But also, and more importantly, Toni after Toni Turek, the greatest German goalkeeper since the war. Toni, a name that made me feel as though I'd been given a title.

1977: FC Cologne win the German Cup Final.

1978: Cologne are Bundeslige champions and winners of the Cup.

1978 was also the year of the World Cup in Argentina. Helmut Schön was the national coach, and Sepp Maier, my idol, was goalkeeper. I would have been deliriously happy if I'd been picked as the number two or even the number three keeper.

'I can stop just as many balls as Nigbur, Franke or Burdenski,' I said in an interview, furious that I hadn't been selected.

Such presumptuousness was taboo. It didn't go down at all well with Helmut Schön, an austere character from Saxony.

'Schumacher? A big-mouth. An adolescent!' was his verdict.

With hindsight, I have to admit that he was right.

Maier was an extraordinary keeper. He played consistently in four hundred consecutive matches. He was reliable. So why should a national coach complicate life by selecting me? And risk upsetting Sepp Maier?

In 1978, after the World Cup in Argentina, Jupp Derwall succeeded Helmut Schön. At first he had the same attitude towards me as his predecessor. My chance came, however. I played half a match in an international against Iceland. And after that, radio silence for a year.

The press kept clamouring for me: 'Schumacher, an outstandingly good player, a great performer, richly deserves a place in the national team.'

Derwell was put under a lot of pressure of this kind. Nigbur was still his favourite. Until that dramatic lunch that Nigbur had with his fiancée. When the meal was over he tried to stand up. Impossible. He couldn't move his knee. 'Trapped cartilage,' was the doctor's diagnosis. The end of a career.

Perhaps the beginning of mine?

Franke or Schumacher? This was the dilemma Derwall was faced with before a game that was to take place in Munich, this time against England.

'I'm going to play in this match, and I'll play the whole ninety minutes!' I announced in the interview.

'The impudence and nerve of the man! He's trying to blackmail me,' stormed the coach, quite beside himself with indignation . . . before he eventually gave way.

The 1980 European Championship Final in Rome marked a real high point. I was lucky enough to have the opportunity of playing and winning with the finest side imaginable. It was young talent – Bernd Schuster, Hansi Müller, Karl-Heinz Rummenigge. There were none of the big-name players, like Overath, Beckenbauer, Netzer. The atmosphere was terrific and team spirit excellent. There was freshness and enthusiasm. Derwall only rarely had to intervene. We became European champions, almost as a matter of course. From then on I was the uncontested number one goalkeeper for the national side. With all that goes with it: the pressure to perform well, the certain knowledge that the number two and number three players are just waiting for the moment when my cartilage goes, or I break a leg, or whatever. You can't exclude the possibility of bad luck. Our fate lies in God's hands. There's nothing you can do about it. Success is like beauty: it doesn't last for ever.

3

THE BATTISTON AFFAIR

WAS IT A foul or not? Was it deliberate, or was it just unchecked aggressiveness on my part? Was it malice, a perverse act of violence, or a spontaneous outburst of resentment and energy combined?

I'm no psychologist or any other kind of -ologist. Nor am I my own judge or advocate. Even today I don't feel that my 'foul' against Patrick Battiston in Seville was a foul. I confess, I still dread looking at pictures of the collision again. Perhaps because I'm afraid of feeling guilty.

My mother saw it on television. A few hours later she spoke to me.

'It was dreadful, Harald. It looked bad, son.'

I accept that, like my mother, millions of people think that I committed a foul. But in all conscience, I don't agree. Of course my character had something to do with it, my uncompromising tackling, my passionate commitment to everything I do.

An eternal struggle of heart over reason.

There are people whose reason always gets the better of their heart. With me, it's the opposite. I've always preferred to make a hundred mistakes listening to my heart, than to be right a thousand times by letting my head rule. I'm absolutely convinced that everything great in life, and in football, is born of passion and not from cool reflection. But as I've grown older, I've come to realize that the promptings of the heart ought to be tempered with a little prudent mistrust. I'm now thirty-two, which is twenty-eight plus four. Four soul-searching years since that collision with Patrick Battiston, who has since become a friend.

Seville. The World Cup semi-final, 1982. France v West Germany. I go into the game feeling supermotivated and concentrating 150 percent.

For me this match was an opportunity, the last chance we had, to restore our image and give the lie to our bad reputation. And also to try to win back our German supporters and the goodwill of the press, which was making us out to be worse than we really were.

The French are playing superbly. They're scoring goals. Some of them kick me and jostle me. There's even one who treads on my hands. The pain goes right through me and I see red. I'm seething with anger. Fortunately, a few dangerous situations give me something else to think about. But these occasional successes cut both ways. Whilst they may calm your anger and aggression, your concentration and motivation go. Success makes you careless. Even though there's a great deal at stake for me in this game: as well as the prestige, it's a passport to the final! It's obviously risky coming off the line. But for whom? The keeper or the striker? You never ask yourself that question. I just have to get the ball away from him. There's no time to stop and think about it.

I come hurtling out from the goal, in the hope of provoking the striker to kick before he's ready. In this kind of situation, the risk of injury is high. For both players.

So I rush forwards. Battiston comes running towards me. I know from experience that he's going to try and lob the ball over my head. I jump up to block it. Patrick doesn't make contact with the ball. It's difficult when you're in the air to put a break on your own momentum. The most you can do is slightly alter course. A goalkeeper's not an aeroplane, after all.

It was too late. I couldn't stop and I couldn't avoid him. I came crashing down on Battiston, with my knees bent. If I'd collided with him head on, it would have been even worse for him. As it was, at the last minute I managed to twist myself round and caught him on the head with my hipbone and backside. He fell to the ground. So did I. I'd also been hit, on the side, but the pain quickly went.

The ball missed the net. A quick glance at the linesman – a keeper's first reaction whenever there's a foul or a collision in the course of play.

Did he have any objection to make? He didn't raise his flag. No reaction on his part. Nothing. Everything was OK. I rolled over, then turned round. Patrick was still on the ground. I walked past him and went and stood on the line.

'You ought to go and make sure he's OK,' I thought. 'You must.'

But two French players, Trésor and Tigana, were already standing there, shouting at me and making threats.

'If I go over there, there's going to be trouble,' I thought.

In order to avoid all risk of confrontation, I decided to stay where I was. I was afraid of what might happen otherwise. I wasn't scared of an argument, nor of the players. But the atmosphere was tense, not to say explosive.

'If you go and apologize now, and they hit you, the situation's going to get out of hand. I'll lose my head and start hitting and kicking back.'

My reasoning was stupid, but who knows? They might well have kicked me, or even spat at me. That often happens. And no one in the stands can see it happening. Getting spat at is the worst kind of insult. It drives you mad, makes you feel murderous.

So I didn't think it wise to go over to Battiston and express my concern. Besides, the match had been far too grimly fought for such a gesture to come naturally to me. I was incapable of going over to him, although that might well have been the simplest thing to do. So my first mistake was not showing any concern for the injured man. I stood in front of my goal, sheepishly kicking the ball around. It was cowardice. Perhaps then, for the first time in my life, I was a real coward.

I wanted to make myself believe that it wasn't my fault. Like a child who's done something really silly and tries to carry on playing as though nothing's happened. I simply refused to believe that it could have been a foul. After all, I had the referee on my side. He wasn't showing me a yellow or red card.

Patrick Battiston was still lying on the ground, being tended to. Inwardly, I was saying to myself: 'Everything's fine. Everything's OK. As usual, he's just putting on a bit of an act to impress the crowd, to win their sympathy, but he'll soon be on his feet again.'

I waited, silently willing him to get up: 'Stand up, man! Why don't you stand up? Hopefully, he'll soon be on his feet.'

A stretcher was called for. The team captains, doctors, orderlies gathered round him. It appeared to be serious. Patrick was going to be taken to hospital.

The referee blew the whistle for the game to continue. Rummenigge came on and scored one goal, Fischer soon got the equalizer; the French didn't know what had hit them. 3–3. Extra time. Then a penalty shootout.

Not content with my earlier exploit, I now had the insolence to stop two penalties. We were through to the final, thanks to my two penalty-saves and my 'foul' on Battiston. Difficult to imagine a more provocative set of circumstances. But I still hadn't taken it all in. It was then, either through ignorance or – not to put too fine a point on it – stupidity, that I made my second big mistake.

On the way back to the dressing-room, I was caught up in the infectious enthusiasm of my German team-mates. We had won our place in the final. And my performance was not unconnected with this victory.

I was inundated with questions, phrased in a way I wasn't used to. Some praised me to the skies, the others were abusive. There was no in-between. Some German journalists, for instance, tried to wind me up:

'Did you know that Battiston lost two teeth?'

'If that's all that's wrong with him, I'm prepared to pay what it costs to have them crowned!'

Far from wanting to make fun of the unfortunate Battiston, I felt as though a great weight had been taken off my mind. I really had been afraid that Patrick might have suffered a head injury, that he might still be in a coma. But the stupid wisecrack had been made. It was very quotable. Proof that I felt no remorse, pity or compassion. I had become the Cynic incarnate.

But yet another pitfall still lay ahead of me. My third mistake was already in the pipeline. In the euphoria of winning, I had completely forgotten about Battiston. No one thought to tell me that some kind of friendly gesture or apology to the injured man was called for. This would never have happened if the officials in charge of the German squad had shown more responsibility, the way it was under Braun in Mexico, for instance. Unfortunately, Rüdiger Schmitz wasn't there either.

At Seville Airport there was another terrible scene. Because our luggage wasn't being checked in fast enough, Paul Breitner, as the man in charge, got stroppy with the airport management and staff. There was a terrible rumpus – lots of yelling and shouting and general aggro. It was real chaos. The German delegation chiefs once again proved to be incompetent. I had no time – and perhaps no desire – to think of Battiston. Perhaps I was trying subconsciously to suppress the memory of my 'foul'. After all, we'd won. We were through to the final.

If the manager of the national team had been at the airport that evening, or Rüdiger Schmitz, they would certainly have taken me aside and given me some good advice. We would have bought some flowers and gone to the hospital. I would have stayed at Battiston's bedside until I'd heard him say that everything was OK. Someone should have taken me to see him. As things were, I was in no condition to think of doing such a thing myself.

Everyone was elated.

'Those penalty saves were fantastic!' some of them said, slapping me on the back.

And they'd no sooner turned away than there were others coming up to me saying: 'Bastard!'

The abuse came from people who had been watching the match on television. In my naïvety, I hadn't given much thought to the impact that the picture on the screen can have.

I was very alarmed by my mother's reaction.

'It looked dreadful,' she told me on the phone.

In the course of a thrilling match – the match of the century, some people were saying – I had been branded a bastard in the eyes of the whole world, without my knowing it. Everyone who had seen the match on television – in France, Germany, everywhere – journalists, specialists, experts, people all over the world hated me. For a few seconds, minutes, hours . . . or for ever.

This reaction was inevitable. Because all these people didn't know me the way my mother, or my wife, or my coach did. The media had given me a worldwide reputation for being a bastard. Worse, a bloody German who had half-massacred a Frenchman. I had joined the ranks of those whose brutality is so often seen in films and on television. I became a political symbol, a role which I was not at all equipped for.

What did I know of history, of the image of the German abroad? Nothing. I was the most apolitical individual in the whole of the Rhineland and yet I had become the symbol of a treacherous German victory over France, a country where anti-German feeling can flare up very easily.

Two players, defender and striker, both try to head the ball. They miss, and head each other. In devastating action replay pictures, you see the impact as their heads meet. The kind of thing you see in the boxing ring. My collision with Battiston had the same effect, so I was told. But my hip was much more resistant than Battiston's face. I couldn't bear to think of Battiston's head absorbing the shock . . . These pictures were shown once, twice, ten times, a hundred times. In ever more detailed close-up, in increasingly slow motion. And the more the viewers feasted on these film sequences, the more intense their hatred for Toni Schumacher became.

The main feature of the 1982 World Cup was my collision with Battiston. The two penalties I'd stopped were
completely disregarded. Both at home and abroad, people
saw me as yet another nasty German. The public had
been fully informed about the scandals at the training
camp at Schluchsee; they knew all about the poor performances, the poor results during training. They had
watched our match against Algeria, our first game in this
World Cup series – we'd lost 2–1. Then there was the fixed
match with Austria. Germans just felt more and more
disgusted with their own team. After Seville, certain journalists felt called upon to name the guilty party once and
for all: Toni Schumacher. I had become the embodiment
of all the German vices: the violence, the brutality, the
harshness, the insensitivity. All this was exemplified by
the 'foul' I had committed in the semi-final. But this was
just a foretaste of what was to follow. Because of me,
Germany was once again discredited abroad. The final
was already lost.

The buoyancy and self-confidence in our own camp was
not great. We ourselves didn't believe we could win. Until
the match with France, we had only turned in weak
performances. The team was far from being in top form.
Certain players – including Karl-Heinz Rummenigge –
were simply not fit and were playing with injuries some of
the time. If only psychologically, we were in no condition
to win the World Cup. Whether or not my collision with
Battiston was a foul, I was in any case a bag of nerves, an
explosive cocktail of suppressed violence, frustration,
mutinous aggression and the determination to win –
despite all the scandals and weaknesses of my own team.
And there was a perfectly logical explanation for all this.

The time leading up to the 1982 World Cup was for me
a real nightmare. It all began with the return of Paul

Breitner to the national side. I was young, I'd only been with the team for a couple of seasons. That the rest of the players should be in awe of old hands like Breitner or Rummenigge seemed perfectly natural. But Rummenigge, a reserved, almost shy fellow, wasn't interested in being a role-model. The one who did want to be top dog and call the tune was Breitner. A fighter with extraordinary charisma, his influence over the team was all the more marked because Jupp Derwall, the coach, had no real authority over us. Breitner, the star of Munich, had such a dominating personality that I never had the nerve to rebel against him. Paul had such a way with words that he was capable of silencing any player, of making journalists look silly, and even openly having a go at Derwall.

On the field, he displayed extraordinary energy, amazing vitality. But unfortunately he wasn't such a good example off the field. He smoked like a chimney, played poker and drank like a fish. And not only did he rule the roost during play and in training, he continued to lead the way the rest of the time as well. It was inevitable that the weakest and worst players in the team should follow his example. It was the easy way out.

The goalkeeper Eike Immel, my reserve, was already addicted to poker. You often saw him pull out a fistful of banknotes from an inside pocket. Or else, if he'd been taken to the cleaners, he would throw himself onto his bed in a fit of depression. The stakes were often as high as 20,000 or 30,000 marks. Other members of the team would live it up until the early hours and turn up for training on their knees.

Others were drinking so much neat whisky they were virtual alcoholics. Breitner almost always joined in on everything, but unlike all the other players, you couldn't fault his performance on the field the next day. He never dropped a pass, or lost a tackle . . . It was crazy. Whereas his drinking companions could hardly walk a straight line, let alone play football. Which was why at the time it wasn't so much Paul Breitner as the others who made me angry. Breitner, a Bavarian, could hold his drink as well as Franz Josef Strauss, the political leader of his native province. Strauss is another one who can drink and party until dawn; and then only a couple of hours later, he'll give a two-hour speech without any notes while everyone else is still in bed with a terrific hangover. That's Bavarian robustness for you!

And that's how it was with Paul and the other players, especially the reserves, who were called 'tourists'. I was shocked and angry. Some of them were thirty-year-old players who knew very well that this was their first and last chance to play in the World Cup. But they didn't let this bother them. They certainly behaved like World Cup novices, but also as though they would have another three or four chances to play in a World Cup side.

I gave Rüdiger a ring: 'Come and get me, I want to go home. What's happening here has nothing to do with World Cup training. It's all hell let loose. The worst chaos I've ever seen.'

This was no exaggeration. Afterwards we'd refer to Schluchsee, where the training camp was, as 'Schlucksee', which means 'liquor lake'.

There was no discipline. The standard of behaviour was appalling. I didn't want to have anything to do with it and spent most of the time in my room.

That was enough to make the others start thinking I was abnormal – how crazy can you get!

What I said to myself was: 'It's up to you to make the effort that no one else will. Especially as you're the only one who wants to win.'

I was only one out of eleven. But nevertheless, there was no denying my ambition. The worse my team-mates were, the better I had to play. This became an obsession with me. And in that frame of mind, I found it hard to recognize the limit of my capabilities, both physical and mental. Unfortunately I'm still the same today. Moderation will never be my strong point. But I'd rather be a world-class player for three years than a mediocre one for fifteen.

But to return to Spain in 1982 . . .

Our 2–1 defeat by Algeria was a painfully mediocre performance. So was our 1–0 victory over Austria. In the latter game because this was the score we wanted. This 1–0 result meant that both Austria and Germany qualified. There was no formal agreement between the Austrians and us over this, but we had a kind of tacit understanding. Breitner had made it more or less clear to me: 1–0 was all we needed.

This kind of thing is no longer conceivable today, since all the matches from the quarter-finals on are played simultaneously. After having scored, we fell back into defence, while the Austrians didn't venture past the half-way line. My finest display of goalkeeping was the result of a pass from a German player. It was laughable. After the match, the crowd of 45,000 waved their handkerchiefs. In Spain, when the spectators at a bullfight do this, it means: 'Go home. You're yellow!'

In this case, the symbolic gesture was addressed as much to the Germans as the Austrians. It was aimed at every one of the twenty-two players who had been more or less strolling around the pitch for the last twenty-four minutes of the game.

I felt ashamed.

Was a German team like this capable of beating Italy and becoming world champions? I didn't think so. And thank God we lost! Which didn't prevent me from making the headlines yet again. Alessandro Pertini, the President of the Italian Republic, complained about me. I had apparently refused to shake his hand. Why should I have done that? How could something like that have happened?

After the final whistle, Italy were world champions. As I've already said, the best thing the losers can do is to remove themselves from the scene as quickly as possible. There's nothing worse than staying to watch the others being presented with the cup. In fact, I think it's perverse to expect the losers to stay and watch.

And because I was in such a hurry to get away, I simply didn't see President Pertini. Otherwise I would, of course, have been very honoured to shake the hand of such a respected and popular man.

A few months later, the Italians lodged a formal complaint with the Ministry of Foreign Affairs. Wolfgang Mischnik, who was then President of the opposition liberal alliance in the Bundestag, and an ardent football supporter, intervened and worked out a solution with the German Football Federation: this entailed a letter of apology and a trip to Rome.

Hermann Neuberger and I were received in the presidential palace by Pertini. It was a real fairytale experience, one of the best moments in my career. A small, very cheerful-looking man came towards me, with his arms wide open, saying: 'Come here and let me hug you, you great sportsman!'

It was extraordinary. We fell into each other's arms like two old friends. The ice was broken. He didn't want to hear any more about apologies, and seemed genuinely delighted to meet me. We chatted together for half an hour about football and about the final in an atmosphere that was completely relaxed. At least as far as President Pertini was concerned, I was obviously not a German villain. It was a real boost to my morale.

At that time millions of people thought I was some kind of wild beast, as I realized as soon as I got back to Germany, although I didn't really understand why.

Perhaps in order to make their defeat easier to bear, the French portrayed me as some kind of mini-Hitler. I was terribly shocked at being cast in such a role. Me, the goalkeeper Toni Schumacher! This was incredible!

No West German Chancellor, no matter how hard he tried, could have generated as much diplomatic controversy as I did.

But I still didn't appreciate the consequences of the incident involving Battiston. I was naïve and no politician. Unlike Rüdiger, my personal manager. He sounded worried when he told me: 'We're going to have to be very careful. In the coming weeks we're going to have to sit tight because there are a few torpedos headed in our direction.'

I cannot feel that I'm personally responsible for the atrocities the Germans committed on the Jews, the Poles, the Russians, the French, no matter how often I'm confronted with those crimes. But who was going to listen to anything I had to say? I was a German barbarian, a hated figure and – if I might be allowed to make a rather provocative statement – I had become a target of a new form of anti-German racism, which flourished on German soil.

I realised that it wasn't enough to tell your own version of the truth. You also had to express it well. This I couldn't do. I didn't know how, and had never learned. All I could do was to turn in on myself.

4

THE MONSTER OF SEVILLE

SEVILLE MARKED a watershed in my life.

Thinking and brooding about my collision with Patrick Battiston had gradually dampened my happy-go-lucky nature. The carefree spirit I had once been became a thing of the past. Toni the joker had suddenly turned serious. I'd always been game for a laugh and enjoyed a bit of excitement, but now I wanted peace and quiet, and to be left on my own. Even music didn't give me any pleasure any more. Something had cracked inside me. I was suffering from an illness that didn't affect the body.

At that point Rüdiger Schmitz made even greater demands on me. He intensified the peace and quiet around me and made my isolation more complete. He accompanied me on long walks again. Just the two of us. For hours on end. Every day. Not even my wife was allowed to come with us. We avoided all contact with journalists. We talked for hours and hours, analyzing everything, dissecting everything.

Rüdiger said very wisely: 'We're soon going to find out who your real friends are.'

He managed to make me see the situation in a slightly less pessimistic light – and to make me accept the idea that I had done something stupid. Stupid, yes, but wicked, no.

We decided that from now on I was going to be very egotistical and in the first place think of myself. I was to concentrate on my football as never before. Immerse myself completely in the game. With the sole aim of repairing my image through my sporting achievements. I couldn't go and shake the hands of millions of people by way of apology, but I could try and gradually win back the public by performing well on the field.

As far as the press was concerned, I harboured no illusions. There are still far too many journalists who are all too ready to make allegations and assertions without really understanding anything or knowing what they're talking about. I'm not trying to justify what I did in Seville. All that I ask is that people should be fair and unprejudiced. The shock of what happened has changed my behaviour. Since then, I try to see every opponent as a man first of all, in every tackle, every clash, every foul. I don't think this has affected my willingness to take risks as a goalkeeper. On the contrary, my own fearlessness often frightens me.

I'll come hurtling off the line with just as much determination and authority as before to tackle any player dashing towards me with the ball. As far as that's concerned, nothing's changed. I know that my collision with Battiston was an accident. But I've learned something from it. The opponent on the ground is a fellow human being I've got to have some feeling for. During the 1986 World Cup I tried to help Sanchez and Maradona. In the Bundeslige I've acted in the same kind of way. It's no big deal. But perhaps no one really wants to know about it. Perhaps a Toni Schumacher who plays a clean game doesn't match up with the image people like to have about me.

In the first Bundeslige games after Seville, I was greeted in the stadium by a chorus of whistling. I always had the same feeling: that the crowd wanted to see me lose, that they wanted to goad me into walking off. They tried everything to unnerve me.

Rüdiger was relentless in telling me over and over again: 'You did something very stupid. Only your performance in goal can help you win the day now and make amends.'

It was these words that saved me and prevented me from succumbing to suicidal self-pity.

At the same time I had to put up with the harassment of anonymous telephone calls and letters threatening to kidnap my children and attack my club. Those responsible weren't French, they were Germans.

Ever since the Battiston affair, I have learned to be more circumspect in my behaviour. On principle, I never make any comment or give any interviews directly after a game. I'm no longer prepared to speak into any microphone held up in front of me straight after a rough game – not until I've had a chance to calm down. Before I can say anything sensible, I need at least to get back to the dressing-room and have a shower. I need a chance to think before I open my big trap. This explains what happened in Munich in 1986, when I was sent off the pitch as a result of a scandalous decision on the part of the referee. I didn't even touch Roland Wohlfahrt (a striker who plays for Bayern) – but I was still shown the red card. For the first and only time in my whole career! Thank God I didn't lose my cool.

Since Seville, I've learned to exercise some self-control at the critical moment. In Munich that evening, I didn't say anything, I simply threw down my gloves, went back to the dressing-room and stood under a shower. Suddenly Rüdiger was standing in front of me. He looked at me and then left me alone. I came out of the shower and looked around for my towel. The match was still going on and we could hear the fans shouting.

'We understand each other,' said Rüdiger as I dried myself. 'Let's say no more about it.'

There was no point in arguing about the referee's decision. Speech is silver, silence is golden. Especially where a referee or Football Federation official is concerned.

Without Rüdiger's help in that difficult period, I would be a human wreck today. But Patrick Battiston's great decency and magnanimity towards me also marked a real turning-point.

Our meeting in Metz a few weeks after Seville was in no way an 'expiatory humiliation' for me. In any case, Patrick would never have condoned any such thing. This trip simply gave me the chance to express the embarrassment and regret I felt for what had happened in the semi-final. It also gave me the opportunity to take some of the heat out of the debate that was raging in France about me, although I didn't fully appreciate at the time just how high feelings were running. Originally Patrick and I had planned to meet somewhere between Metz and Cologne, and to celebrate our reconciliation with a good meal. But Patrick wanted to offer a journalist friend of his, who worked for a Metz newspaper, the exclusive story of our meeting. He promised me it would be very low-key affair.

So the three of us set off: Rüdiger, his brother Karl-Josef Schmitz who was going to interpret for us, and myself. I was a bit worried. How was Patrick going to react?

When we got to Metz we were shown through the back entrance of the main offices of one of the local newspapers. The front entrance was besieged by television crews and photographers. Patrick's journalist friend was waiting for us.

'Patrick is upstairs,' he said. 'He's expecting you.'

I followed him into a small office. Then Patrick arrived.

He spoke only a little German, but understood it pretty well. I told him my version of our collision: the high cross, the way I came out of my area, the ball bouncing, my feeling that he was going to lob the ball over me.

'That's how I saw it as well,' he said.

I told him as forcefully as I could: 'Listen, Patrick, I never had any intention of hurting you. Never, I swear. That's the last thing I was trying to do.'

'I believe you,' he said. 'It's just as I thought.'

I think I had tears in my eyes. He was still wearing a surgical collar round his neck. The impact of our collision had inflicted serious cervical lesions on him. What a relief this meeting of ours in Metz was to me! Patrick had been extraordinarily decent. I was still responsible for the terrible pain he suffered. But this didn't prevent him from showing great generosity and not holding what I had done against me.

'Come, let's shake hands,' he said. 'Perhaps we can even become friends now. As far as I'm concerned, Seville belongs to the past. It's finished and done with. Let's not say any more about it.'

This handshake was a great moment for me. A very happy moment.

'Would you have any objection to having a photo of the two of us taken? My journalist friend is waiting.'

'OK, Patrick,' I agreed.

I had no objection. We were taken upstairs and into

another room. It was just the way you imagine Hollywood to be. There were dozens of photographers, microphones, cameras, projectors, yards of cable. An unpleasant surprise. As much for Battiston as for me. It was far too hot. There wasn't any air. I was cross and irritable. I could feel the veins in my head swelling, ready to burst. I felt as though we were cattle being driven to slaughter by the media butchers. I felt very angry.

Patrick sat down beside me, facing the mob of journalists, with Rüdiger and Battiston's journalist friend on either side of us. We were chatting together, but already a guy had flung himself under the table with a microphone. Rüdiger, in a tone of voice that was nonetheless friendly, said: 'Now get away from here, do you hear?'

The guy extricated himself from under the table.

They wanted to know all about our meeting. I explained that Patrick and I had already talked together, and that everything was OK. That I had told him how much I regretted what had happened, how sorry I was, that I hadn't intended to ... etc, etc. Another handshake. All very Hollywood. A blinding explosion of flashbulbs.

The *Bild am Sonntag*, the major sensationalist Sunday newspaper in Germany, had also sent a journalist along. A real witch. Right at the start of this circus, she'd dropped a word in my ear: 'When this is over, come along with us. We'll have a little something to eat and take a few photos. OK?'

'Never,' I said curtly. 'No way.'

From that moment on, that harpy was out to get me.

There were a few awkward questions that Battiston and I fielded, protesting the sincerity of our reconciliation, even if it was too early to talk about friendship at that time.

Yet another handshake. Yet more photographs. As though we were film stars.

'I'd like to go now,' I said, getting to my feet.

I was soaked in sweat.

But the 'journalist' from the *Bild am Sonntag* wasn't going to let us off so lightly.

'Do you think,' she went on in her fluty voice, 'that you're going to mend Franco–German relations with this handshake?'

My reaction was spontaneous.

'I didn't ask you to come here. I don't need you as a witness or to photograph my handshake with Patrick. I came to apologise to him: it's a matter we've sorted out between ourselves. I'd rather not comment on your disgraceful behaviour. But are you crazy, or something? What do you expect me to do? Am I supposed to jump out of the window for the sake of a Franco–German reconciliation?'

'But what about relations between the two countries?'

What kind of trouble was this hag trying to stir up, clawing open old wounds that were barely healed? I couldn't stand the sound of her shrill venomous voice a minute longer. I needed some air. All I wanted was to get out of that room. I could have accepted and answered any tendentious or hostile questions from the French journalists. But they had been polite and civil to me; of course they hadn't been particularly friendly, which was understandable, but they'd been fair and sympathetic.

Naturally, my reaction immediately prompted murmurs of disapproval. What kind of trouble had I got myself into now!

On the way back, my companions and I drove for at least an hour in silence. We could already visualize the headlines in the papers the next day: 'Schumacher makes a scene'; 'Another Schumacher rumpus in France'; 'Angry outburst at scene of apology.'

I felt powerless. Once the media have branded you a monster, you don't stand a chance against the press. There's no point in protesting. The only solution is to cut yourself off. No more interviews, no more comments, no more television appearances. All you can do is to make sure you don't give any cause for criticism in your performance on the pitch. But this attitude of mine was also misinterpreted. The media were angry with me for remaining silent. They were prepared to pay me a fortune for an exclusive interview. Newspapers, magazines, they were all interested, all desperate to hear what I had to say. What they expected to hear, I still wonder to this day.

My only aim was not to make any mistakes in goal. It wasn't long before the press was saying: 'Schumacher is a block of marble. He's cold and insensitive, and only comes alive when he's in front of the net. That's all he lives for.'

I didn't laugh any more, stopped going to parties, and even avoided club functions. I just kept my head down: I'd get in the car, train, shower, and go home again.

Rinus Michels, my coach at the time, was sympathetic: 'What happened in Seville was an accident. It could happen to any player. But what's past is past. You ought to forget about it.'

At Cologne, the other players were careful not to revive any painful memories. Seville was a taboo subject for them. I found their consideration very touching.

Peter Weiand, the President of FC Cologne, also did his best to help me. During a dinner with friends, at his home in Cologne, he tried to persuade me in all seriousness that Patrick was entirely to blame for the collision in Seville. I found this slightly amusing, but it did make me feel a little better.

What was my day-to-day life like? Psychological harassment, headline stories, even alleged blackmail attempts. The gist of most of these was: 'If you don't give us an interview, we'll give you a really hard time and a much worse press.'

Whatever you do, don't make any mistakes, Harald. Don't let a single ball in, Harald. Make sure they can't criticize you for that.

This was my only response to these attempts to intimidate me. The only response I was capable of. In retrospect, I might well have cracked up under the strain. At home, I was just a bundle of nerves. It was certainly very hard on my wife, Marlies. She even suggested we leave Germany at one point. She was marvellously supportive all through this critical period.

'I'm right beside you. Even though you may have done something silly, without meaning to.'

All the same, the Battiston affair was a subject we always avoided, and the same is true to this day.

Does time heal wounds? Does it calm anger? Does it stifle hatred? Only in part. Will the French ever forget? Will they ever forgive me? These questions were uppermost in my mind at the time of a FC Cologne v Paris-St-Germain match that I had to play in France . . . a match that I wanted to play. I wasn't going to be a coward and stay behind in Cologne.

In Paris the crowd roared and whistled and shouted. Fortunately it was a small crowd. This is perhaps why their display of hatred didn't seem so terrible to me. I wasn't really aware of the feeling on the terraces.

At the airport it had been quite the opposite. As soon as we landed I was greeted by security police and escorted to the stadium via a different route from the rest of the team. The police had taken the murder threats against me very seriously.

'Bloody hell!' I said to myself in the car. 'What on earth must the French think of you?'

I felt like a dictator who needs protecting, or a criminal who has to be closely guarded.

But Paris was just a foretaste of what was awaiting me on 18 April, 1984, in Strasbourg. A friendly match had been organised between France and West Germany to mark the opening of the new La Meinau Stadium. All 45,000 seats had been sold.

'A test for Schumacher'; 'What the public feels in the run-up to the European Cup'; 'How will the German team conduct itself in the match against France?' The press whipped up the tension before this match by presenting it as a kind of French revenge match after their defeat in Seville. Revenge against the Monster Schumacher, as well as the German team. Just as in Paris, 'the monster' had to be protected from the crowd. There were policemen everywhere – on the coach, at the hotel, at the training ground. It was unnerving. But I wasn't afraid. Fear is a bad counsellor – I knew that from childhood.

The day of the match. I got on the coach. The back seat on the right. Curtains closed. The Walkman headphones pressed down tightly on my ears. Peter Maffray. His song: '. . . Kill me, it's the only way you can be sure I won't fight back any more.' The title of the song: 'Revenge'; it was perfectly in keeping with my state of mind.

On the way to La Meinau Stadium, I caught sight of some banners carrying hostile slogans and a few swastikas being waved around. Once again I was the Nazi, the warder at Dachau. I didn't want to see or hear any more. I drew the curtains tightly shut and returned to Peter Maffray.

What did people want? Were they after my blood? Was

it the final death-blow they wanted to see, as though I were a bull in the ring? Why?

At the hotel Rüdiger and I had analyzed what I was up against.

'You either let them get to you, or you ride it. You must win over the crowd. If you don't tame them, they'll tear you apart like wild animals. You must have the courage to go out on the pitch, alone, half an hour – perhaps even a little earlier – before the match begins. That way you can let the first explosion of hatred discharge itself, and show them that you know they want to destroy you. Go and stand in your penalty area looking like someone who expects to be lynched. But don't forget the most important thing: you have absolutely nothing to fear, you're quite safe. There are police all along the railings. You'll be met with a wall of hatred, of unbelievable intensity, unprecedented hostility. Take it all in. Don't close your ears to the whistles, don't hide. The venom they feel must come out.'

It was quite clear what was at stake; if I played badly, I'd topple into the abyss. I'd be finished. At least as far as playing as an international was concerned.

My place in the team was not in any case guaranteed. Jupp Derwall had already tried to get rid of me. He had selected Bernd Franke, the number two goalkeeper, to play in a match against Munich. But Bernd had been very decent about it.

'I'm not going to play in Toni's place,' he'd said. 'He's still the best. I'm thirty-two. Soon be retiring, the end of the road . . .'

Derwall had given way. After the game in Munich, he had to give me credit for my performance. But in Strasbourg he was nervous and anxious. Never the glimmer of a smile on his face.

The other players tried to show their solidarity in their own way.

'You'll be all right,' they said, as much to reassure themselves as me.

In the dressing-room, changing. I could already hear the hum of the crowd in the stadium; it sounded more menacing than a swarm of angry bees. The time was slipping by too quickly. Already it was time to warm up. Warming up means going out and showing yourself. I had to go out there. Accompanied only by Horst Köppel, who was going to give me some practice shots in goal, we went out, as planned, half an hour before the other players.

There are ten steps that lead you right out into the middle of the stadium. From the bottom of the steps I could already see the blue uniforms of the policemen outside armed with long truncheons. There were riot police everywhere.

I was still at the foot of the steps. I looked round and took a deep breath.

I've got to go up now.

Hörst Koppel asked me: 'Where are we heading for?'

'Right into the lion's den,' I replied, as though in a trance.

I wanted to get it over with. For the sake of my team, and for my own sake, the crowd had to purge itself of its fury. I had to tear myself away from the obscurity of this corridor and go out there into the light.

Suddenly I emerged from the top of the staircase. There's tremendous shouting and whistling. Schumacher stands alone on the pitch. There's no Frenchman, no other German player with him, just the Monster of Seville.

If it weren't for the police and the railings, there's no question they would tear me to pieces.

I run up to the half-way line then start running towards the goal. I'm showered with eggs, potatoes, tomatoes, stones. The whistles of the crowd are more piercing than the scream of fireworks going off. The air vibrates with the noise. Countless missiles are thrown down on me.

I could open a canning factory on the spot. The avalanche of vegetables just keeps coming, as well as bottles and tins. I continue running diagonally across the pitch towards the goal. I always run up and down the pitch six or eight times before beginning my warm-up exercises. I do the same this time.

I go and stand in front of the net. The crowd, the photographers, the television cameras and the journalists are all behind me. The dirty looks from the press are harder to take than all the rotten eggs that get me in the small of my back.

I do my warm-up exercises. Horst Köppel waves his arms around, trying to quieten the crowd. The roar only increases, and gets wilder.

'This is unbelievable!' shouts Köppel. 'Would it be better to stop now and go back?'

'Never!' I yelled. 'If I go now, they'll think I'm chicken.'

I felt certain – I just knew – that when they stopped shouting the Seville affair would be laid to rest. I had to brave it out. I had no choice.

The other players finally appeared on the field. The anger and hatred from the terraces had died down a bit. The match could begin. I was in excellent physical condition and my concentration was perfect. Above all, I wanted to prove that I was a good goalkeeper. So I played well. My first chance to show what I could do came after five minutes' play, and after that there were several opportunities for some difficult saves.

After one of these, Battiston came up to me. We winked

at each other and he gave me a friendly tap on the shoulder. A gesture that said a lot. Patrick obviously didn't like the fact that the crowd was continuing to hold against me what had happened in Seville. I responded likewise to let him know that I'd understood.

Half-time. Of the 45,000 angry spectators, there were now no more than 20,000 still whistling at me. The others had already dared to applaud some of my better saves.

At the beginning of the second half, I went back out onto the pitch at the same time as the rest of the team. There was no need now to go out alone.

Every time I intercepted the ball, I noticed the crowd's readiness to applaud. After nearly two hours – I had come into the pitch at good half-hour before play began – the hoped-for turning point came: out of the crowd of 45,000 who had hurled abuse at me at the start of the match, there were only 5,000 die-hards. The others were impressed by my performance and acknowledged it. As it happened, the French won the match 1–0 – a totally unstoppable goal. Does winning make it easier to forgive? Victory makes you magnanimous.

Rüdiger was right. Only my game, total concentration on my game, could help me weather the storm.

On the way to the dressing-rooms, Patrick Battiston made a point of coming up to me and shaking my hand. He congratulated me on my 'superb saves' and suggested we swop shirts.

'Not here,' we agreed. 'It'll look as though we're just doing it for show. In the dressing-room, OK?'

A few minutes later the exchange took place. For me, it was a marvellous moment. Rüdiger stood apart, observing the scene. Then we hugged each other.

I knew this was an important moment in my partnership with Rüdiger Schmitz. Our side had lost 1–0, but

– forgive the egocentricity – for me it was a real victory.

The next day the press were unanimous in praising my game. In France as well as Germany. There was no mention anywhere of the Battiston affair.

It was wonderful, fantastic, extraordinary.

Only one paper, the *Welt am Sonntag*, did not join in the chorus of praise. The report it contained was signed by a certain Mr Golz, Karl-Heinz Rummenigge's best friend, apparently. I've never exchanged a single word with this journalist, but for years he's had it in for me. He's always criticized me. Strasbourg was no different. The article concluded by saying that Schumacher should make way for Burdenski, the keeper who's supposedly going to succeed me.

That's what you call fair play.

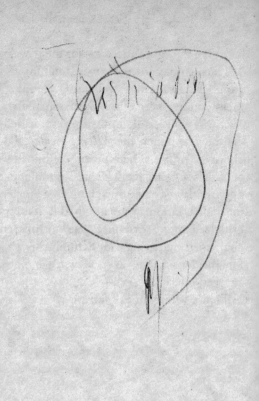

5

RUMMENIGGE ALONE AGAINST THE MAFIA

The Galinda Mansion, a luxury hotel. The accommodation was great, the organization left nothing to be desired. And what's more, the man in charge was Egidius Braun, who was a father or brother to all of us, depending on our need.

In the morning, a half-hour jog in the forest before breakfast. At eleven thirty: an hour's training, which took us up to lunchtime, followed by a kip in the afternoon. Another hour's training before supper. In the evening, we could listen to music or read. There was a holiday atmosphere – apart from one or two minor problems.

During training, Hans Peter Briegel, the star of Verona, was getting on my nerves. We'd been divided into two teams, A and B. Hans Peter was playing with as much energy as a Sicilian who'd been woken during his siesta. With him on their side, team A were losing every match.

'What's wrong with Peter? Why's he so lethargic?' I asked Felix Magath.

'It's disgraceful!' said Felix – Peter's apathy had not escaped his notice.

'Just look at him! His mind's on anything but his opponent. He's out for lunch. Useless!'

In terms of training and form, the poor fellow had got too used to the good life in Italy. He still managed to pull himself together for the important matches, thank God – though he must have taken huge doses of vitamins to do it.

Compared with the shambles the 1982 World Cup in Spain had been, the 1986 event in Mexico was a rather well-organized affair. If one of the principle participants, our coach Franz Beckenbauer, had managed to assert his authority more effectively from the start, everything would have gone more or less perfectly.

I would no more dispute Beckenbauer's 'technical know-how and instinct for the game' than Hermann Neuberger, President of the German Football Federation. And certainly we owe it to Beckenbauer that German football is no longer on a downward slide but climbing back up again. But in Mexico, Beckenbauer was overwhelmed by the weight of his responsibilities. Perhaps that was the reason for his constant irritability? He would explode at the least provocation, and kept putting his foot in it. At a press conference where he was asked to comment on the departures of Littbarski for Racing-Club of Paris and of Förster for Marseilles, he replied incredibly tactlessly. He regretted the loss of these players, and said: 'The Bundeslige is left with just the dregs.'

Another of his rather undiplomatic statements was: 'We'll never become world champions with a team like this.'

After giving us a verbal thrashing by sounding off to the press, he got the whole team together in order to apologize. I looked him in the face and realised that he hadn't meant any harm, and I had to laugh.

'Don't look at me like that!' he said in an angry tone of voice. 'There's no need for sarcasm. We understand each other perfectly.'

He knew that I had been critical of his methods, ever since we were at the Kaiserau training camp. Franz had selected twenty-six players, of whom only twenty-two were to travel to Mexico. As you can imagine, this was bound to cause friction. An experienced boss would have considered the psychological effects of a situation like that, and discussed the matter with the longest-serving players, such as Felix Magath, or Karl-Heinz Rummenigge. Beckenbauer might also have remembered the time when he himself was playing for the national side.

The voice of wisdom and experience should have advised him against anything of the sort. He ought to have known that it was virtually impossible, or in any case extremely difficult, to make twenty-six players live together for two weeks, when they know that at the end of the day four of them are going to be dropped. The atmosphere in the training camp was inevitably miserable. Uncertainty was poisoning the players' hearts and minds because only one thing was clear: of the twenty-six players there, only fifteen could be 100 percent sure of their place in the squad; the other eleven were waiting to find out, in a state of anxiety, impatience and mutual distrust.

I too was affected. During the preliminary match against Holland, which took place in Dortmund, it was Uli Stein that Beckenbauer picked to replace me in goal.

I had a discussion with Franz about it.

'In my opinion,' I said, 'the team that goes to Mexico should be used to each other, have experience of playing together.'

'You're right, Toni,' my coach admitted. 'But on the other hand, we need to let new players in. If only to try them out.'

'It's a bit late for that now, isn't it?' I said. 'You should have thought of that sooner.'

'I had no choice, Toni. In my view anything's still possible. Every player here ought to have a chance. Including Uli Stein, the reserve goalkeeper. Don't take it as any reflection on you if I tell you to sit on the sideline from time to time. Just for once. You'll survive.'

'Tell me honestly, Franz. Am I under pressure from Stein?'

'No, everything's OK. But I'm the one who makes the decisions.'

'True. But I still think that the team that's going to play in Mexico ought to get used to each other. I've got to get a rhythm going with the libero. So it's as much in the team's interests as my own that I'd like to play at least half a match with the new libero in Dortmund.'

'You're being obtuse,' said Franz angrily. 'Stein must have a chance to prove that he's capable of being a good number two, and that's all there is to it. I'm the one who decides, not you. The team will have plenty of time to play together. As has always been the case.'

Weeks later, in Mexico, Beckenbauer was full of praise for the French side's superb teamwork. The result of playing together for a long time. So my arguments weren't all that stupid. I myself had given Franz the opportunity to put his decision into practice. My little girl had been taken to hospital with pneumonia. I asked the assistant coach Horst Köppel for time off. Franz was violently critical of my absence. Worse still: he took advantage of my concern over my little girl's illness and used it as a pretext for 'letting me off' the match against Holland and replacing me with Uli Stein. This was a lame excuse. The discussion about what for me were the crucial advantages of having a team with experience of playing together started up again. I had aired my opinions on the subject very freely in the press. Which gave Franz the opportunity to read me the riot act in front of the whole squad: 'If you don't like it here, you can go home.'

In the end that's just what I decided to do.

Hermann Neuberger immediately got in touch with Rüdiger Schmitz. Rüdiger came to see me. He managed to persuade me that it would be a mistake to go. It was in the team's interests as well as my own that I should stay. Beckenbauer was the first to be informed of my change of mind.

'I'm going as well,' I told him.

'Where?' he said.

'To Mexico, for the World Cup.'

'Where else did you think you were going?'

'Home. I wanted to go home. As you well know.'

'You crazy fool!' he said, laughing, wanting to play down the incident. 'But I never had any intention of dropping you, Toni. The thought never crossed my mind.'

This to-ing and fro-ing was very disconcerting. It unnerved me. If Beckenbauer had been as tough with me in Mexico as he was at Kaiserau, we could have saved ourselves a lot of trouble. Exchanging the role of player for that of coach is no easy thing to do, and Franz hadn't yet made the complete transition.

'Franz can blindfold me next to a one-hundred yard drop and tell me to walk step by step towards the edge, and I'll do it. I have complete confidence in him. I'll do whatever he says.' This is the original transcript of an interview I once gave.

I still have unquestioning faith in Beckenbauer, but

now I'd take a little transmitter with me, so that he could shout 'Stop' at the last minute.

No, that's not what I really think. I would hope, though, that instead of being a one-hundred yard drop, it was just a couple of feet.

The other person causing the team problems was one of the players on whom our greatest hopes depended: Karl-Heinz Rummenigge. He wanted to show the international press in Mexico that he was still a top-flight footballer, and that his legendary control of the ball could still be relied upon. Despite all his injury problems. And despite his thirty years (a critical age for a striker, as everyone knows).

Karl-Heinz was suffering from a strained leg muscle that had given him trouble in 1982, in Spain, and again in 1984, in Paris. But this time it affected him mentally as well as physically. He was obviously suffering from a persecution complex. Franz Beckenbauer made this very significant comment about him:

'He has eyes and ears in the back of his neck, which allow him to see and hear the grass growing behind him.'

Karl-Heinz himself said later:

'It's impossible to prove what people are feeling. I've had to learn this from experience. There are looks, gestures, silences, whisperings behind your back. It gets worse and worse – but you can't ask anybody about it. You would be making a fool of yourself if, for instance, you were to say to Toni: "Why do you look away? Have you got something against me?" He'd just join in the laughter. Some journalist friends of mine told me things that some of the Cologne players were supposed to have said about me. In the magazine *Bild*, they told me, there are some unpleasant remarks about you. And in the Cologne *Express* Toni says that you're not in the team. In the evening at the press conference, I lost my temper. I hit back: "It's all a conspiracy on the part of the Cologne Mafia." An hour later Toni had heard about it and we had a row in the hotel dining room.'

And that's more or less what happened. It was almost bound to happen. With hindsight, I realize that a player as discontented as Karl-Heinz Rummenigge was bound to flip his lid sooner or later. For him I was the most high-powered player, so it was me he wanted a confrontation with. If he won, that would confirm his position as leader in the team hierarchy, which was what he needed to boost his self-confidence. His moodiness can't be put down solely to his injury. Even if he'd been in good health, if he'd had all his strength and technique and speed, Rummenigge would still have found some way of causing us problems. Like all great stars, he's inspired but he's an egotist. He wants everyone to pander to his wishes, and adapt themselves to suit him. Otherwise, he moans and groans, but never openly, never candidly. That's where he's wrong.

The number of times he's come up and complained about Beckenbauer's training methods, about the senseless jogging we do, and about the disastrous atmosphere within the team!

'Come on, then,' I finally said to him. 'Let's go and talk to Franz. That's the best thing to do.'

We set off: Felix Magath, Karl-Heinz Förster, Rummenigge and myself. Everyone was quite open with Franz about their grievances and made suggestions for improving things. All except one person: Rummenigge. He remained diplomatically noncommittal, betraying none of his feelings, never raising his voice. His first angry words came much later – directed against me.

That Rummenigge should play the clever tactician was

certainly surprising in the circumstances, but it didn't really surprise me. Once before, at the time of the World Cup in Spain, I'd got wind of a tacit agreement between Rummenigge and Breitner, whereby neither would in any way criticize the other. This alliance enabled them to silence most of the team. Only Uli Stielike had the courage to speak up and openly criticize Rummenigge's attitude:

'Whoever's injured and can't play ought to let someone else take their place in the final.'

It was impossible to get this idea into Kalle's head (Kalle being Karl-Heinz's nickname). In his overweening conceit, he thought he could still play better football than anyone else even when he was injured. That's what happened in Seville in 1982, and it was the same all over again in Mexico, four years later. I know what he went through to try and recover from his injury in time for the competition. But despite all his efforts, he did not regain his form. He was never 100 percent fit. Unfortunately, he didn't have the elementary decency to say early enough: 'I'm sorry, I'm not going to make it. Take a player who's fit. Forget about me.'

Franz believed in him. He was always giving Rummenigge another chance. 'Of course, you'll be coming with us,' he would tell him, in the hope of boosting his morale.

But these promises simply made Rummenigge more impatient.

Uncertainty and indecision are the breeding-ground for lies. I have a better understanding today of what was happening then: Karl-Heinz was afraid I would take his place as captain of the team. Personally, I really wasn't interested in being captain. There are too many hassles that go with the job. Everyone feels entitled to come along and have their little moan – it would get on my nerves. This obsession of his was no doubt planted in his brain by some well-meaning 'advisers'. Perhaps the journalists on the *Welt am Sonntag?* In any event, somebody led him up a blind alley by telling him whopping great lies, deceiving him into thinking that he was better than the other strikers Voller, Allofs and Littbarski, and that the team was solidly behind him. Whereas in actual fact Karl-Heinz was really not very popular. In Mexico he managed to upset everyone. The 'Rummenigge problem' was even raised at a meeting of players: he was arriving late for every meal, he'd commandeered the services of a masseur round the clock, when there were only two masseurs for all twenty-two players. As it was, they didn't have time for everybody; with Karl-Heinz monopolising one of them, the rest of the team had to made do with the other. Everyone had to fend for himself, and not say anything. I nearly always had to change the bandage on my strained Achilles' tendon myself. This didn't bother me too much: I knew that Kalle's injury meant that he had special training to do that was very painful. We would all have welcomed a third masseur, but even to bring up the subject was regarded by Karl-Heinz as lese-majesty. Chronically hypersensitive, Kalle became withdrawn, and very chummy with the Munich player Augenthaler and Stein, my rival from Hamburg. Perhaps it was these two players who drummed into him the puerile notion that I bore a grudge and hated him. Why? On account of the two goals he had scored for Inter Milan in the match against Cologne in the European Cup Final. This was ridiculous. The allegation that Kalle and I were at cross-purposes upset me.

'Toni and I have never been friends,' said Karl-Heinz in Mexico.

This wasn't quite true. After all, I'd invited him, along with twelve other friends, to my wife's birthday party.

And I'd been a guest at his house on Lake Como, in Italy. I really didn't have anything against him. Only against the German Football Federation (the DFB).

It annoyed me that the DFB should treat us differently. Rummenigge was asked to write an occasional column for the *Welt am Sonntag*. He was allowed to sign a contract with them. But I wasn't given permission to do something similar: the Cologne *Express* wanted me to write a kind of daily chronicle. But I didn't get the approval I needed to go ahead with it.

The way the tables were arranged in the Galinda Mansion indicated anything but harmony amongst the players. Beneath the watchful eye of the 'Holy Trinity' sitting at the coaches' table – Franz Beckenbauer, Berti Vogts, Horst Köppel – everyone was divided into three clans:

– the Munich clan, which included Hoeness, Augenthaler, Rummenigge, Matthäus, as well as all the reserves, who were sick with frustration, and a couple of 'Northerners', such as Stein and Jakobs.

– the Cologne cell, with Allofs, Littbarski, Immel, Rolff and myself.

– and the others, including Förster, Briegel and Allgower.

The groups were an expression of the players' degree of independence and autonomy, of their likes and dislikes for one another; they were little enclaves where like-minded players could meet and relax.

During training, I had to give Stein practice in goal. He had openly declared himself to be my rival, but I managed to ignore his jealousy and deep-rooted hatred of me. But not being a masochist, I certainly didn't want to have to put up with him at the table. I preferred to have a friendly chat with 'Litti' and Allofs. Clearly, our splitting up into little groups didn't do much for team spirit.

Quite the opposite. The atmosphere was poisoned with suspicion and mistrust. One evening at dinner, I noticed unusual excitement and murmuring at the Munich table. We on the Cologne table didn't know what it was all about, and sat there completely unsuspecting. As usual Pierre Littbarski quickly finished his meal, and left the room. He reappeared two minutes later. We were expected in Rüdiger Schmitz's room. That was all he said.

So we went up to Rüdiger's room via the back stairs, and were given a detailed explanation of what it was all about: 'The Cologne Mafia.' What an idiotic expression! I was furious. Outraged by such an unfair accusation. I'd always been scrupulously fair about Karl-Heinz in interviews, and always said: 'If Rummenigge is fit, he must play. If not, he shouldn't be on the field.'

I was fully aware of his ambition, and what torment he put himself through to get back to the peak of his form. He was determined to be a star of the World Cup. The Argentinian Maradona, the Frenchman Platini, the Mexican Sanchez – all the greats, and Karl-Heinz wanted to be counted as one of them. And if he had been, I would have been genuinely delighted. He had the engine running, but for him the flag hadn't gone down yet. He was still on the starting-line whilst the others were already on the circuit. He was sick with frustration and now he was spitting poison and bile in my direction.

I exploded.

'That's it! Enough's enough! I've had it up to here! I'm going home!'

Rüdiger tried to calm my indignation.

I telephoned my wife, Marlies. She shared Rüdiger's opinion: 'Neither Rummenigge nor Stein are worth giving up your chance to play in this World Cup. You've worked hard for this for four years!'

Klaus Allofs and Pierre Littbarski were as shocked and angry as I was.

'That son of a bitch!' shouted Allofs. 'He limps round the pitch like a lame duck and now he wants scapegoats. The guy's only got himself to blame. This can't go on. We've got to say something.'

'Quite right,' said Pierre Littbarski. 'Kalle's lost his marbles. Which isn't surprising, he's under so much pressure. The press and the public expect too much of him. But the fact that he's started talking rubbish is no reason why we should punish ourselves by pulling out of the competition. Rüdiger's right. We can't blow our chance of going to Mexico and playing in the World Cup just because of that ludicrous statement Rummenigge gave to the press. That would be crazy!'

'There's no question of my wanting to pull out either,' said Klaus Allofs. But we're going to get Karl-Heinz to retract this Mafia twaddle in front of Beckenbauer, Braun [the head of the German delegation] and everyone in the team.'

Allofs and Littbarski were no less angry than me. I found the whole thing extremely distasteful. Pierre Littbarski managed to get hold of Beckenbauer on an internal telephone in the hotel restaurant. Franz was pretty annoyed and asked us to come down.

Some people become aggressive when they know they're in the wrong. Karl-Heinz is one of them.

'Stop bad-mouthing me in *Bild*, *Spiegel* and *Express*,' he yelled. 'You're jealous because I'm captain. I know you are!'

'You're completely crazy!' I said.

Franz Beckenbauer can testify to the fact that I'd already turned down the captaincy when it was offered to me at Kaiserau.

'Let's go and find the newspapers,' said Rummenigge. 'Then we'll see who's crazy and who's lying.'

Pierre Littbarski got hold of the relevant papers; we got *Der Spiegel* telefaxed from Germany. And then the search was on. There was nothing. Not a single disparaging word quoted as coming for me – in any of the newspapers. My name wasn't even mentioned in *Der Spiegel*.

Rummenigge wasn't going to give up though. He just wouldn't let go. He couldn't prove anything, but reading between the lines, he sensed there was an implied suggestion . . . He was relying solely on his impressions and assumptions as grounds for picking a quarrel.

At first it was just embarrassing, but then it became extremely annoying. Even for our coaches. For the first time ever, Franz gave Rummenigge a dressing-down, in our presence – without much success. Karl-Heinz just kept on repeating: 'Toni has turned everyone against me.'

'That couldn't be further from the truth, goddammit!' I shouted in fury. 'Up until now I've been telling all the journalists that you must play. Now stop all this nonsense and apologize. I'm not going to put up with your offensive behaviour any more. I'd rather leave!'

'I don't believe you,' he went on stubbornly. 'I have the feeling . . .'

I stood up. 'Oh, stuff your feelings. I've heard enough about them. It's just a waste of breath trying to prove I haven't done anything to you.'

Rüdiger was waiting for me in his room.

'It's no use,' I said. 'I'm not having any more to do with it. It's all a lot of drivel. The next thing, someone will be up here with the explanation that Rummenigge hadn't meant to suggest that it was quite so much of a Mafia – although it is a bit of Mafia . . .'

Franz called: would I go and see him in his room?

'Forget it, Franz. There's just no sense in it. I'm not going to put up with being slandered. I'm going home.'

I went to my room to try and calm down. I put on my keeper's gloves and started lifting weights. Up, down, up, down ... until I was exhausted. I was bathed in sweat when Felix Magath and Rudi Völler came into my room. They both wanted to persuade me to stay. I wouldn't even consider it. Why should I have to put up with Rummenigge's moods and unpleasantness? Völler appreciated my point of view.

Then Beckenbauer came storming into my room and had a go at persuading me to change my mind. 'Come over to my room. We're all waiting for you.'

'No.'

Franz spent the next half-hour preaching in the wilderness. I obstinately refused to say anything, lifting my weights, up, down, up, down, silently wishing I could throw them at him. How could he be so weak, so bent on conciliation, so horribly diplomatic. Yet again. I detest this kind of diplomacy. Franz clearly wanted to spare Rummenigge the embarrassment of making a public apology.

Felix Magath, normally a discreet and sensible individual, was seething with indignation. Before the World Cup he was greatly criticized. His superb performance in Mexico had restored his self-confidence; he could give his opinion and know that it would carry weight.

He told Franz in no uncertain terms that he considered him as one of the people largely responsible for this dismal spectacle, because he hadn't used his authority to insist that Rummenigge behave reasonably.

'We've had a bellyful of Karl-Heinz's antics, and more than a bellyful of this ridiculous Mafia story,' said Felix angrily. 'Toni's right. Is Rummenigge playing or not? I suppose that yet again you won't want to talk about that right now.'

This attack coming from one of his most loyal supporters came as a deep shock to Franz. Feeling that he'd been backed into a corner, he struck out at me: 'If you don't stop lifting those goddamned weights, I'll throw the wretched things out of the window!'

He was helpless with rage and I felt for him. My anger gradually subsided. 'You can hardly lift them, let alone throw them,' I said, grinning at him.

He grinned back. We exchanged a few more friendly insults, then I followed him to his room. Allofs, Litti, Vogts, Köppel, Egidius Braun and Rummenigge were waiting for us. Braun fiddled around with the wording of Rummenigge's apology. But Karl-Heinz remained as stubborn as a mule.

'I can't say that,' he groaned. 'It makes me sound as though I'm not my own man.'

Braun wasn't having any of it. 'Now that's enough, Karl-Heinz. This can't go on. You're going to apologize now, otherwise we'll have to do something about it.'

In this face of this threat, Kalle finally said he was ready to withdraw his accusations. After a last attempt to find an acceptable formula.

'Victory for Schumacher!' people said afterwards. In what way? I hadn't wanted any fight or argument, so there was no defeat or victory as far as I was concerned. It was all a waste of time, just a bit of unnecessary childish nonsense.

Two days later Kalle himself agreed. After a photo-call, he asked if he could have a word in private with me.

'Have you got a moment?' he wanted to know.

'Of course,' I replied, delighted with his overture.

'You know, Toni, we've had it out with each other. This

silly business seems to have been settled. But it isn't really. We're avoiding each other, and we don't have anything else to say to each other apart from "Good morning" and "Good night". The rest of the team can see that the two strongest personalities in it are still at daggers drawn.'

'You're right, Karl-Heinz. And I don't like it either.'

'So let's forget the whole thing, shall we? For the sake of the team!'

I was pleased that Kalle was prepared to put the interests of the team above his own. For the first time since I'd known him. You have to hand it to him! After the armistice, we'd finally signed a peace treaty. The press talked of a reconciliation. At last.

I don't really want to go delving into Karl-Heinz Rummenigge's psyche, but I believe that he's trapped in a vicious circle. After all, I'm under the same pressure to perform well, I know the fear of an injury that will make us unfit to play ever again, one that means goodbye to our careers and any contracts, an end to our popularity, and the threat of financial difficulties hanging over our heads like Damocles' sword.

Rummenigge's biggest sponsor after Adidas is Fuji. It's as clear as crystal that Karl-Heinz must have signed a deal with them worth at least one million marks. After all, he was a football international and a potential World Cup finalist in 1982 and 1986. He felt morally and professionally obliged to play if he possibly could. I'd done the same thing in Rome in the 1980 European Cup when I played with a broken finger. What would have happened if I'd let one or two goals in?

It's an enormous responsibility. How would Inter Milan have reacted if his image had become tarnished? Perhaps there were also penalty clauses in his contract with Fuji. I don't know. But I've always been against penalty clauses. Clever publicity executives always try to include them in the contract, specifying for instance that the footballer must play in a European or World Cup match, or win the Bundeslige championship, or score a certain number of goals during the season, and so on. I refuse to sign any such clauses, on principle.

6

MEXICO

I'VE NEVER considered Karl-Heinz Rummenigge an enemy. This cannot be said of Uli Stein, the number two goalkeeper for the German team. There is no longer any possibility of the two of us getting along together. Originally, I didn't want to waste so much as a line on the guy, but I wouldn't like people to misinterpret my reticence as cowardice.

Stein is exceptionally well versed in dirty tricks; he usually aims to land his punches below the belt. The ambition to come first is perfectly normal and absolutely legitimate. I can sympathize with it. But Stein believed that all he had to do was to slander his rivals often enough and he would achieve his aim. I cannot sympathize with his continual calumnies.

Stein is a very good goalkeeper, I freely admit. But I don't expect him to say the same about me. But he'd be doing himself a favour – as his own credibility only suffers as a result – if he didn't make such completely negative remarks about my capabilities.

His presence in Mexico was hard to endure. I asked the assistant coach if I could train out of sight of this hate-filled 'team-mate' Stein, and away from his poisonous presence. Horst Köppel was very understanding and agreed. But this attempt on my part to stay out of his way was not enough to quieten our number two keeper. He continued to disseminate hatred and resentment. Not even Beckenbauer was safe from Stein's venom: Stein called him a really vile name. This led to his quite rightly being chucked out of the team and sent back early to Hamburg before the rest of us.

His departure was a great relief to me. Even the other players who had shared a table with him suddenly regained their usual friendliness. They came up to me, clapped me on the shoulder and congratulated me: 'Great! That was a superb save. Keep it up!'

Beckenbauer's angelic patience with this mass of character deficiencies continues to baffle me. Perhaps he behaved with such exemplary forebearance because, according to various statements in the press, he had good reason to know that Stein, Hoeness, Augenthaler and Jakobs had stayed up three whole hours after lights-out. And there were the craziest stories going round about women at the Galinda Mansion . . .

But there's another explanation that seems to me much more plausible. Shortly after he took over as manager of the national side, Franz took me aside:

'I'd like you to be captain of the team.'

I was amazed. The title belonged to Rummenigge. As time went by, Franz realised that I had a fairly strong personality. Did he want Stein to act as a counterbalance to me, someone I could pit myself against? Stein must have realized what was going on. Did it make him resentful? Is that why he started spreading those silly malicious stories about me? With impunity!

During half-time in the match against Uruguay, he lay down on the pitch and pulled his jersey up and let the sun burn him. He seemed to want to get sunstroke. Completely irresponsible behaviour. Who would have replaced me in goal if I'd been injured?

Stein watched the match against Denmark from the terraces – 'from on high'. What he forgot was that even on a Himalayan peak, a dwarf is still a dwarf. Stein will never get another chance. There's too much trouble when he's around. Will Immel be my successor? Why not? He's talented. Perhaps he's still a bit too inconsistent, too immature. But he's got plenty of time. And I'm not ready for the scrapheap yet.

Communal life is one of the most difficult styles of living, so it's said. Are conflicts and quarrels inevitable? Let's allow ourselves to dream a little: imagine that an international game is about to take place. All feelings of rivalry, frustration and friction between the players are thoroughly aired and talked through. Thanks to the excellent group dynamics, all problems disappear during the preparatory training period. How much greater is everyone's motivation because of the harmony in the team? How much greater are their chances of winning?

In the years remaining to me, I would like to force myself to become a little calmer. Perhaps I'll learn to keep myself in check. I'm often too direct, too outspoken. If I don't like something, I'm incapable of responding tactfully or diplomatically. Franz Beckenbauer doesn't approve of this. Probably because he has a similar character. He too says silly things that he has to retract the next day. He's a Bavarian, after all. And I'm from Cologne, where we shout even louder.

In spite of our quarrels, and all the mistakes we made, on balance Mexico wasn't a total disaster. Not from a sporting point of view, at least.

The first game: Germany v Uruguay. The South Americans play a hard game. They have an English style of play combined with a Latin temperament. We were outclassed. The heat almost killed us. The result, a one-all draw, was a real miracle!

Second match: Scotland v Germany. This was no easy game. And the same oppressive heat. We were useless in the midfield, and our forward line was slow and spiritless. After being a goal down, we finally won 2–1 with considerable difficulty.

The Danes were quick, active and athletic. And they gave us a good lesson in the game. These football wizards from Copenhagen know how to put their opponents off their stride early on in the match. Their German trainer Sepp Piontek has done a good job with them. A 2–0 defeat for us.

We were really worried before the game with Morocco. If they won by one goal, Morocco would be through to the next round and we'd have been eliminated. We'd have sooner played against a strong team than an unknown outsider. We scraped through with a 1–0 win.

That hell-hole Monterrey: Germany v Mexico. The whistle blows for the start of play. The crowd goes wild. All hell is let loose. I wouldn't be surprised if the referee allowed himself to be influenced by the tense atmosphere. But he remains objective and neutral.

I don't have much to do in this game. A few minutes before the end there's a dangerous header. I just manage to deflect it over the crossbar. I was lucky. The whistle goes for the end of the match. The score 0–0. The reserves come running up to me.

'Well done, Toni, that was a great save. You saved the

match for us with that last one. I thought that ball was already in the net,' Rudi Völler congratulated me.

Then to encourage me: 'You're still the best! You'll stop at least two of the penalties. You're bound to. You can do it! I'd stake my life on it!'

The crowd is roaring and shouting. The Mexican fans beat their drums. The noise is deafening. It's just what I need. I'm in my element in a situation like this. I need a challenge. I'm always having to prove myself, and take on a superior opponent – this is a pattern that runs all the way through my life. Not allowing myself to be put down.

Mexico lose the toss – their goalkeeper has to go first. Allofs scores. 1–0.

My turn. The Mexican places the ball and takes a few steps backwards. There's a roll of drums behind me. I see the striker come running towards me, nearer and nearer. My feet leave the ground and I plunge to the left. Negrete, the Mexican, shoots the ball to the right. 1–1. I fall into a black hole, defeated. But I'll get the next one!

Brehme shoots even more decisively than Allofs. 2–1.

Now I'm back in goal. The next Mexican striker is Quiarte. Don't react too soon, Harald. You must wait until the very last moment. Wait! Like a jumbo-jet at the end of the runway before take-off, with all its engines going but with the brakes still on, holding back a moment.

The ball comes to the centre. I'm already flying off to the right but I still manage to get my knee there and deflect it.

Matthäus takes the next one: 3–1.

As though in trance, I stop the next penalty. Pierre Littbarski takes us to 4–1. I don't understand why our team has suddenly exploded with joy. Pierre jumps on me.

'Well done, Toni. You've won. We –'

'Shut up. I still have to . . .'

'You don't have to do anything more! The match is over! It's over, do you hear? We're through to the semi-final!'

It's true. That great little guy Pierre is right! 4–1 to Germany. A three-goal lead. The Mexicans can't catch us now.

However, I couldn't rejoice unreservedly. I knew how important a Mexican victory was to the crowd, I realized how disappointed they must be. I still had in my mind images of the unbelievable poverty we'd seen outside the stadium. Football was synonymous with hope. A form of escapism that had now been taken away from these people.

A cause for celebration and sorrow – that's how I saw it.

Rudi Völler ran over to me, overjoyed. For him, as for the others, I was King, Kaiser, God, Hero of the Day. I felt proud, but I didn't overrate my contribution: I'd only dotted the i. Without the rest of my team, I'm nothing.

Before we played against France, I'd watched the superb France v Brazil match. A wonderful game. Lots of one-twos. Tackling that was textbook perfect. Spectacular shots. Only one weak point: defence. Live and let live. Play and let play. Latin elegance. Beckenbauer's verdict on the Brazilian game: 'If we have to play against them, it'll be easy. They have one big weakness: they like to play an attractive game. That's what they're used to, and they let their opponents play in the same way. All we have to do is break through early enough in the game and they're finished.'

The same went for France, who had something else going against them: their football stars from the 1982 World Cup and the 1984 European Championship were older now, and not so dewy-fresh. Wolfgang Rolff had no trouble in neutralizing Michel Platini, which meant that the French eleven's rhythm was destroyed.

Afterwards, I heard a great deal of talk about the French

team's psychological block in the face of the 'brutal Germans'. Stuff and nonsense! Rubbish like this has little to do with sport, but perhaps a lot more to do with the inability of hacks and politicians on either side of the Rhine to come to terms with the past. Sport is being used as a screen on which old clichés and prejudices are projected.

This is all too complicated for me! We won in Seville because the French underestimated us after establishing their 3–1 lead. We won in Mexico because we adopted the right tactics: harrying our opponents, in order to put them off their stride from early on in the match, and not giving them room to play.

We did not take the Cup back to Germany with us. Which made our triumphant welcome in Frankfurt all the more surprising. There were 15,000 supporters waiting to greet us outside the Town Hall. We were delighted. 'We're proud of you,' Dr Moog, the Mayor of Frankfurt called out from the balcony, when the team came out in front of the jubilant crowd.

Kalle wasn't with us, so as vice-captain I had to speak: 'The reception you've given us does the heart good. I'm proud to be able to play for Germany. I'm proud to be German.'

Thunderous applause. I certainly touched a chord. I subsequently received huge quantities of mail: 'At last, someone's prepared to talk about national pride!' 'Bravo! There's nothing shameful about loving one's country!'

Have we Germans finally reached the point when we no longer feel we have to apologize for being German?

One thing became clear to me that day: I would have to be careful what I said in future, and how I behaved. As members of the national team, we represented Germany – whether we liked it or not.

I've always been one to go butting my head against a
brick wall, with all the intelligence of an angry rhinoceros.
Even a wall made of reinforced concrete. It is well known
that wisdom comes with age, and I see things a little
differently now. We all have to make concessions sooner or
later. So I don't turn down invitations quite so systematically any more. If, for instance, the DFB (German Football
Federation) decides that we should visit an orphanage, I'll
go along too, with the rest of the team. Willingly, in this
case. Sport has an important social role to play in the life of a
country. For some people, football acts as a focus for their
nationalist fervour and they see the game as symbolic of a
battle between warring countries. This is regrettable, but
unfortunately almost inevitable. Football and nationalism
both date back to the nineteenth century. How much of a
coincidence is this? Even today, only a minority of people
regard it as unimportant whether their country wins or
loses. Football has a political dimension. The flood of
letters I received after my public address on the Town Hall
balcony is proof of the fact.

Before it was organized and specific rules laid down,
football was a competitive game for children. When a pig
was slaughtered in the village, the children used to run after
the bladder, and they would all try and get hold of it. This
ritual part of the kill enabled the kids to let off steam and
work off their pent-up aggression.

To this day, football continues to provide a kind of
release, though in a more disciplined, regulated way.
However, there may be spectators who would like to see the
players tear each other to shreds . . .

People's aggression is often transferred onto sporting
contests and this is relatively harmless. The feelings of
violence and brutality are largely under control. Nationalism and chauvinism undoubtedly persist, and continue

to inspire our fans. But not so much the players on the field. I bet that despite all the nationalistic fervour on the terraces, not 5 percent of the spectators would be prepared to die for their country. They much prefer to die a hundred sporting deaths in the course of an exciting international – through us acting as intermediaries. It's better than going to war. Not everyone who comes into the stadium thinks only of the sport. But then not everybody who goes to church thinks only of God.

Chauvinism in sport is, generally speaking, harmless. The winners win without having to pay a heavy price for it, and it isn't the end of the world if you lose. Looked at closely, a victory is the sum of lots of little individual battles.

To this day, I've never been ashamed of being German. I was proud to receive well-deserved praise after a good performance. I sing the national anthem without the least inhibition – for me, it's always a fairly moving moment. I'm very grateful to my country and am happy to live in a society in which sport acts as a springboard that has enabled me to become a somebody, and to earn my living decently, in fact royally. And for that reason, I shall continue to pay my taxes in Germany, unlike Boris Becker and others. I'm a patriot, but not a nationalist.

7

SEX AND DOPE

IN THE AUTUMN following the 1986 World Cup we became embroiled in a stormy controversy. The cause of the debate: the excessive medical care lavished on the team in Mexico.

I complained in private about the neglect we suffered, being left to look after ourselves, after weeks of excessive medical care at the hands of Professor Liesen and his medical team.

Perhaps it didn't do us any harm to have the team with us – considering the conditions in which we had to play, at that altitude and in that heat. And the local standards of hygiene were pretty exotic. But the whole 'health programme' we were subjected to seemed to me excessive, and indiscriminately and haphazardly applied.

It began with the three litres of mineral water with added trace elements that we had to drink every day. The reason we were given for this sounded credible enough: extraordinary physical exertion causes the body to lose too much electrolyte and mineral salts. It seemed logical to make up for this deficiency. So all the players duly drank the mineral water, though not always very willingly. After the third day, we all had diarrhoea. I think this was because it was served to us far too cold.

Every lunchtime we took a large quantity of pills with our electrolyte mineral water: iron, magnesium, a vitamin B concentrate, vitamin E, and a few altitude tablets. Next to the table where I sat with Klaus Allofs, Pierre Littbarski and Wolfgang Rolff, was a palm standing in a wooden tub filled with earth. In about two years' time, there'll be nails growing in it, I imagine; to a man, we carefully planted all our iron tablets in that tub. It was all very well being told afterwards that the red blood corpuscles need a great deal more iron to compensate for the reduced levels of oxygen at a higher altitude, we just couldn't take so many chemicals.

Our diarrhoea might also have been caused by the large doses of magnesium we were given, so I was told by a doctor friend of mine in Cologne, who was just as sceptical as I was about the huge quantities of medication.

'I would never take more than ten pills a day,' he told me. 'You just can't tell what taking all those different pills at the same time does to the side effects – it might make them weaker or stronger.'

The purpose of taking the magnesium was to prevent cramp from muscle tension – although according to expert medical opinion, this is just an old wives' tale.

Apart from the pills, we were also given injections the whole time. Professor Liesen himself administered some three thousand injections.

These contained everything imaginable: plant extracts to build up the body's immune system, high doses of vitamin C and B12, extract of bees' honey to stimulate the heart and circulation, extract of calves' blood for altitude

problems. And on top of that, vitamin E tablets. I felt this
was just too much. Except perhaps for the run-down
'Italians' amongst us – Briegel and Rummenigge – who
were used to less frequent and less demanding training
sessions than we in the Bundeslige.

My distrust of his pills deeply upset Professor Liesen.
And Berti Vogts was most put out because I refused to
take part in his 'little runs' after training. But I had to do
as I was told. It was all part of the sports doctors' myth-
ology and Vogts insisted on it: it was supposed to help
reduce the amount of lactic acid in the body.

For my pains, I got myself an inflammation of an
Achilles' tendon that played me up for six weeks.

But all the same, the tests continued to show that my
lactate count was higher than that of the 'sprinters' on
the field. It's no wonder: I'm a goalkeeper not a marathon
runner. But I was still strongly advised to do half an
hour's jogging in the woods every day.

The medical supervision did not, of course, stop on the
threshold of the dining room. Our diet included lots of
meat, potatoes, pasta, water and fruit juice. Pierre Littbarski had to give up his favourite drink, Coca Cola. And
whilst at home I'm a real connoisseur of chips and
hamburgers, pork chops and home-made stews, I now
had to be content with a selection of glucides, lipids,
vitamins and carbohydrates.

Though my stomach was rumbling with hunger, I
refused to bow to this collective diet. Already in 1985, on
our first acclimatization trip to Mexico, I'd rebelled
against it. I preferred to eat nothing but fried eggs and
salad for a whole week! And to drink just mineral water
and the occasional beer in the evenings. All the other
players had diarrhoea for the whole trip. The only healthy
one of the lot was me!

During the 1986 World Cup I didn't touch a piece of meat for six weeks, having learned my lesson from experience.

The Professor was always lecturing me about it: 'Toni, you're being quite impossible. What about your carbohydrates? Don't be unreasonable!'

But I wouldn't give way. My worried team-mates repeated what the Professor said: 'Harald, this is sheer insanity. You can't go for weeks. . .'

'Why not? I feel fine. Leave me alone.'

Dieticians are no doubt very nice people; their well-meaning advice is commendable. But they ought to be more tolerant and admit that there are exceptions. There's no such thing as absolute truth – and that goes for the sportsman's diet as much as anything else.

In 1986, the former tennis champion John McEnroe was trying to make a comeback. To regain his form, he nibbled away at a 'healthy diet'; muesli, milk, etc. and never took his eyes off his table of calories. He was bursting with health. Felt very good. But was totally unsuccessful. In his heyday, he took no notice of the dieticians' carefully calculated menus. And on an unhealthy diet of icecream and hamburgers, he used to win.

I've never had any time for sleeping pills. I absolutely refuse to take them.

Liesen told me: 'They're indispensable, because a player who's slept well feels much better.'

This wasn't a good enough reason, as far as I was concerned. If I can't sleep. I prescribe myself a glass or two of beer. And I can be sure of sleeping like a well-fed bear.

After initial disapproval, everyone resigned themselves to my special treatment. At Kaiserau training camp, I once asked our assistant trainer Horst Schmidt for another beer. He turned quite pale, looked around furtively, and whispered in Berti Vogts' ear. My request was categorically turned down. Not for long. I became rather angry. And after drinking my hard-won beer, I then slept like a baby.

The sportsman's needs as regards eating, sleeping and sex are either ignored or overcomplicated. The mental and sexual isolation before and during an event perhaps bothers me less than most of my team-mates. The opportunity I've been given of perhaps becoming world champion governs my life for four to six weeks. My family steps into the background. If they were nearby, I'd find it more of a worry than a joy.

I see it this way: Mexico is 12,000 km from Germany. Let's suppose that, like Rummenigge, I took my wife and children with me and installed them in a hotel near our training camp. One of the children could have fallen ill — something which could just as easily have happened at home. But from a distance it wouldn't have been so worrying. It would have affected me less. After all, I wouldn't have been able to fly back and forth 12,000 km. But if my child were lying nearby in a hotel bed with gastric flu and a temperature of 40 degrees, then I wouldn't have left his bedside and couldn't have played football.

I understand players, like Karl-Heinz Förster, who don't want to give up their married life. 'I want my wife with me,' says the former Stuttgart player, now with Marseilles.

And why not? As far as I'm concerned, his beloved can even sleep with him. If it means he plays better the next day, we all benefit.

It's better to be pragmatic about these things than stick rigidly to principles. I detest generalizations and regimented behaviour. I enjoy sex as much as the next man, but I certainly don't need my wife with me during such an important competition as the World Cup. So I do without sex. After all, I'm no gorilla.

At times like this, I shelve my love-life and concentrate on my ambition: to become a world champion, the best goalkeeper in the world. I don't have time for pleasure or desire.

Whether consciously or unconsciously, these feelings are channelled into the will to win. 'Sublimated', as my friend Dr Callenberg explains: 'By channelling your natural impulses, emotions and drive into the right sporting effort, you can realise a far greater potential than the sexual act.'

I share his opinion. I'm in favour of abstinence. And in favour of concentration on the particular sporting objective. In any case, many wives of players refuse to accompany their husbands on trips as a sexual convenience. They object to it as undignified and degrading. 'We're not going along just to be screwed!' they say. 'And no one thinks we're there for any other reason. Everyone thinks: "Aha! he's got his beloved with him, they must be rutting all night!" '

Anyway, it's impossible for a couple even to think of living a harmonious conjugal life when we're under such enormous pressure to perform well on the field. It's just asking for punishment. No. It would be better to employ the services of a callgirl if necessary. That way there wouldn't be any general absolute ban on women. If any player wants to have a woman in his room, he should be allowed to. He should just make sure he doesn't disturb the people trying to sleep next door.

This kind of problem doesn't arise in the Bundeslige. We set off for our training camp on Friday afternoons, play on Saturday and are back home by the evening. I can't imagine that any of our footballers are such sexual athletes that they can't go one evening without making a woman happy. Most of us manage to get through twenty-four hours without a woman.

But when the training period is longer, the management of the Football Federation ought to allow players to stay in the same hotel as their wives, though for myself, I would rather leave Marlies at home.

Sex often gives rise to a lot of whispering and grinning and meaningful silences. Players behave like a bunch of adolescents, when they ought to be brave enough to discuss these matters openly. We're not eunuchs. Why shouldn't we avail ourselves of a callgirl, as long as she's been checked by a doctor? Each to his own preference – blonde, brunette, red-head – in the certainty that the girls are clean. It would be better to organize this kind of encounter than to have the boys sneaking off to the next town to some filthy brothel and picking up a dose of the clap.

Imagine the alternative: Egidius Braun or some other official informs us that there are a dozen pretty girls sitting at the hotel bar. Whoever's interested takes a quick look and makes his choice . . . and gets a good shot of penicillin afterwards. He gets his sex with only one risk: that of having his eyes scratched out when he gets home.

The present situation is as absurd as it is hypocritical: we live like monks but never stop boasting about our Don Juan prowess. A football international can have as many women as he likes. As long as he gets a hard-on, it's all the same to him how the lady comes to be in his bed. Is it on account of his green eyes, his muscly arse, his shapely footballer's calves? Or is it his Casanova ways that have made the ladies weak? He doesn't give a damn. The important thing is that he should get his sexual satisfaction.

It's inhuman to insist on weeks of abstinence; it goes against nature. The most sensible solution would be to call on the services of professional prostitutes.

A postscript on the excessive medical attention we received: at the end of the September 1986 we were in Copenhagen to play an international friendly match against Denmark.

Professor Liesen got wind, from the press, of my criticisms of his methods. He was upset about it.

'I must speak to you, Mr Schumacher,' he said crossly.

'Of course, Professor, whenever you like. Here and now, if it suits you; I'm listening.'

'I'd rather hear straight from you any reservations you have about my treatment than read about them in the press.'

'I never intended that you should. I simply aired my views among friends, in private conversation. I wasn't seeking any kind of publicity for them.'

'I find it nonetheless deplorable that people should get the impression that you . . .'

'It was not my intention to attack you, or question your competence, or undermine your reputation. Had I wished to do so, I would have got an expert scientific opinion on the matter. But I do think that it's no coincidence that the game of all those who played in the World Cup has gone to pot, that those who went to Mexico are not giving a very good account of themselves in the Bundeslige today. They've got no energy. And I stand by my critical remarks: after being overtreated, we were given no treatment at all. We were pumped full of stuff in Mexico and then abandoned.'

'Because you didn't ask for any help or advice,' Professor Liesen protested.

This was a ridiculous reply. How can I be my own

doctor? How am I supposed to be able to diagnose accurately the causes of my depressive lassitude?

You can combat pain and overcome your doubts, but there's nothing you can do about lassitude. The human body, this near-perfect machine, has its limitations, it gets worn out, so that it's no longer equal to the daily demands of a competitive life. A natural exhaustion sets in. Otherwise, it would be capable of ever greater performances. Good medical care – even excessive care – can help a little. But the temptation to resort to artificial remedies increases.

A major risk facing sportsmen is that they lose their grip in situations of stress, and become dependent on drugs.

This is already a well-known hazard in the cycling world. The word 'dope' has been common currency in that sport for decades, with the number of doping scandals too many to count. Amphetamines, anabolic steroids, hormones . . . everyone's heard of them, and efforts have been made to bring this plague under control through systematic tests.

Dope in football? Is such a thing quite unthinkable? Unlike cyclists, footballers don't have to undergo a urine test after a game – except in a World Cup or European Championship match. If there's no test, the problem doesn't exist – that's obvious, isn't it? But there is doping in football circles – naturally, it's a closely guarded secret and completely taboo.

I admit quite candidly: I tried out a medication that had doping effects, during training. The drug was called Captagon.

Various cough mixtures containing the substance ephedrine are favoured by players. Ephedrine, as I discovered, heightens aggressiveness, increases levels of endurance and bolsters the ability to fight back.

But the after-effects are bad: you overreach the body's limitations, indeed you completely overtax yourself. Over a period of time you use up your biological capital. Without any checks, without the body giving any of the warning signals that you rely on to tell you: 'I can't take any more!'

Then for days afterwards you're completely exhausted. And despite being so tired, you can't get any sleep to recover your strength. And as far as making love goes: you're completely useless. Not the slightest stirring of virility.

From this experience I learned that repeated use of drugs not only puts your life in danger, but it's also degrading. So don't touch them!

It's the middle of the night and I'm wide awake. I'm staring at the ceiling with my eyes wide open. I'm hot and cold all over. Every muscle in my body is aching.

After the European Championship in Paris, in 1984, I did something very stupid. Out of curiosity. To test the limitations of my own body, I resorted to artificial stimulants. I wanted to force my body to exceed its 100 percent level of capability and to perform doubly well. I wanted to know how far and for how long you can overreach yourself. On top of which, I was injured and worried about the physical condition I was in – I was anxious about the obvious wear and tear on my muscles, my tendons and my bones.

I was under terrible pressure, with incredible demands being made on me, and always teetering on the edge of depression. And I gambled with my health – abusing the machine that is my body, like a racing driver gone mad who overtaxes his engine. Though all the warning lights are flashing and the rev counter's showing 9,000 to 10,000 revolutions a minute, he accelerates! I was aware of the risk that I might eventually seize up completely. It was crazy, irresponsible, insane.

The doctors had warned me of the after-effects of these stimulants but I wanted to find out for myself: I wasn't content any more with just sugarlumps as a source of additional energy.

And I still don't regret having taken them. I was after all my own guinea-pig – although guinea-pig isn't really the word for it: I felt more like a locomotive, always going at full steam – in training and before warm-up sessions for various Bundeslige and Cup games.

Was I an isolated case?

Cologne. Autumn 1984. Once again the club management talked of a critical match. Once again, it seemed, the survival of the club was at stake. Several players tried out various different stimulants – gulping down cough mixtures that contained the highest doses of ephedrine, quite indiscriminately. Then fortified by the drug, these colleagues raced up and down the field like the devil incarnate. We won. But at what cost? After days and days of feeling completely drained, we resolved never again to turn to drugs! And not one of us will ever be tempted to be so foolhardy again.

But my Cologne friends and I are certainly not the only ones who were unable to resist the temptation of dope. Dope is something of a tradition in the Bundeslige.

When I was a very young player, I used to act as chauffeur to many of the established football stars of FC Cologne's senior team. I've frequently driven half a dozen of our great players in my little yellow R5 to a Cologne doctor, where they collected their pills and injections before an important match. Even at the time, it struck me as odd that such healthy individuals should need to pump themselves full of medication like that.

Some of them could hardly envisage any continuation of their careers without these special high-performance pills. Pills and their performance – these had come to mean the same thing, for them, and they could no longer imagine their lives without stimulants.

One important detail: this doctor was treating these celebrated players at a time when doping was beginning to hit the headlines. I suppose that his special medication consisted of anabolic steroids, amphetamines and various other stimulants.

There were footballers in the national side who became world champions thanks to the effects of chemicals. One of them was a Munich player whom we nicknamed 'the walking chemist'. He had a little knowledge of medicine and tried out all kinds of special concoctions on himself. If you were to take a close look, you'd find a clear link between doping and the extent of injuries among players. Torn muscles are very often a sign that a player is on drugs, because they rob you of the ability to sense and appreciate your own limitations, so it isn't surprising that the muscles and tendons don't stand up to the strain. The body's warning system is disconnected. Is it any wonder then that the muscles should go on strike?

All forms of dope are a poison. So my advice is leave well alone. I know that unstable personalities are more at risk; people must be informed of the dangers and preventive measures taken. After all, if you put a 500 horsepower engine in a Volkswagen 'Beetle' you won't get very far.

8

THE SPECTRE OF INJURY

FOOTBALL IS NO sport for sensitive youths; it's for great strapping fellows capable of taking a pounding.

In professional football a player is above all a big investment. Illness or injury puts him out of action and leads to financial loss. The footballer is therefore under constant pressure and obligation to be able to play. The temptation to use drugs to make a player who's unfit fit is considerable. Doctors and players often feel pressurized by managers and coaches. A torn knee ligament takes eight to twelve months to mend. Coaches regard six months as sufficient time for recovery.

I live in constant dread of injury that might make me unfit to play for a long time. Because, until now, I've always succeeded in persuading myself that pain is a figment of the imagination. I have so far been able to ignore the damage to my bones. Sepp Maier still remains my role-model. Despite numerous injuries, he continued to play brilliantly in over four hundred matches, without missing a single game.

I've a deep cut on my knee – I carry on playing, just gritting my teeth. Afterwards: into hospital for half a dozen stitches. The following Saturday I'm back in front of the net. I can't bear whinging. Until now, I've always been able to forget pain.

1980: the European Championship in Rome. I dived for the ball during training and fell badly on my hands. There was a sinister crunch. The immediate swelling confirmed my fears: I'd broken the third finger on my left hand, putting my hand out of action. Keep cool, and keep quiet about it, Toni. If Derwall and the team doctor get wind of your injury, they'll send you straight back home. The reserve goalkeeper Franke is just waiting to replace you. And what guarantee do I have that my place on the national side will still be waiting for me afterwards?

I told no one but Rüdiger Schmitz about my misfortune. We had a talk about it in my hotel room. Soon we were huddled over a drawing, designing a special goalkeeper's glove with a plaster cincture built into it, to keep my broken finger bound to the middle finger so that I'd be unable to move it. Would it work?

Rüdiger immediately set off for Metzingen, the town in Bade-Wurtemburg where my gloves are made to measure by a man called Gebhard Reusch. He understood the problem at once. And in record time he'd made two pairs of special gloves, one for dry weather, the other to wear if it was wet. With the precious items in his luggage, Rüdiger flew back from Stuttgart to Rome.

The European Championship Final: the broken finger didn't let us down. Nor did the rest of Toni Schumacher. We became European champions.

Jubilation and elation. After our victory I finally told Derwall and the other officials. Amazement on their faces gave way to dismay, relief and finally appreciation.

They besieged me with questions. Had I been aware of the risk I was taking? Hadn't I been afraid of not being able to get away with it?

'The only thing I was afraid of was breaking another finger in today's game,' I said with a grin, feeling relieved and certain that I was to remain the number one goalkeeper.

As far as I can remember, I've always had to play in spite of any pain. Torn muscles, cartilage operations, reparatory surgery during the holidays. It usually happens like this: on Saturday I play the last game of the season, then on Monday I climb onto Professor Schneider's operating table in Cologne. After two weeks in hospital, I have a week recuperating at home. Until we start training again. Only in this way can I be fit for the first game of the new season.

'You're number one! And that's where you've got to stay! It means everything to you. You mustn't give the number two any chances to dislodge you from that position.'

Friendship, rivalry . . . jumping at opportunities . . . hoping that your rivals will be injured. Such is a goalkeeper's destiny.

Battered bodies; not a square centimetre that hasn't been knocked, kicked or taken some form of punishment. A modern gladiator? Your bones may crack – but you must play on! You have to take all kinds of risks, there's no holding back. Unfortunately, I'm not as lucky as someone like the Italian goalkeeper Dino Zoff who has a great defence to stand behind. My very close friend Jean-Marie Pfaff, the Belgian international who plays for Munich, is also better off than I am from that point of view. He can quietly carry on thinking of himself as the best goalkeeper in the world – for what can disturb the proud oak tree? But I don't have it so easy.

In Professor Schneider's opinion, I'm the exact opposite

of a model athlete. For years I've been suffering serious damage to the ligaments in my knees as a result of a sporting accident. This really serious complaint is commonly called a 'loose knee'. The situation is made worse, in my case, by the fact that I am knock-kneed, which is symptomatic of a congenital weakness in the knees. My joints are very overworked, and the strain on my ligaments is considerable. I really need to be operated on urgently, but the outcome of the operation is not foreseeable. For the time being, the only acceptable solution for me is to be careful. Professor Schneider says: 'I could operate. But without any guarantee of success. And it would require months of complete rest. But we could also try something else: to compensate for the weakness in your ligaments I'll devise an intensive exercise programme for you. You must exercise your quadriceps – that's to say, the bunch of muscles above the knee – so intensively that they can hold your knee-cap in position. It's lucky that you're so keen on exercise. You should be able to do it.'

Professor Schneider knows that I train until I drop; he knows the extremely high demands I make on myself. He also knows how stubborn I am in working myself. I slave away, exercising until I'm half-dead, just like Kurt Bendlin, the German decathlete, another of Professor Schneider's patients. Sometimes the good doctor asks himself why we do it.

'For Bendlin, pain is a work of art. He only feels really happy after a gruesome physical ordeal. Training for him is like a drug. It's a religion.'

This applies just as much to me. I remain stoic and impervious to pain under treatment. I prefer radical to gentle methods. I'd far rather a quick injection than a tedious massage. Is this masochism? Or self-punishment?

*F*lying high:
Schumacher takes
to the air during a
friendly match
between Cologne
and Arsenal in 1981.

*T*he moment of
impact:
Schumacher and
Battiston collide
during the 1982
World Cup Semi-
Final.

Karl-Heinz Rummenigge, pictured here during the 1984 European Championship, has pointed the finger at Schumacher more than once.

The West German team line up before the 1986 World Cup Final in the Aztec Stadium: (from left to right) Rummenigge, Schumacher, Briegel, Jakobs, Berthold, Forster, Eder, Allofs, Brehme, Magath, Matthäus.

Schumacher is left stranded as José Luis Brown (second from right) heads in Argentina's first goal in a 3-2 victory.

Because I earn too much money? Because I've dropped my childhood friends? Because I put Battiston into hospital? Three good questions – that are impossible to answer. Only one thing is certain: my obsession with training is a means of self-assertion. 'Self-gratification,' Rüdiger would say, when he's in a bad mood.

Among footballers, including football internationals, there are always a few who, like children, have slightly sadistic tendencies. In training camp, there's been at least one madman who has heated his teaspoon in a candleflame until it was white-hot and then pressed it on the arm of one of his fellow players, just as cattle are branded in a Wild West film! And all the victims of these notorious 'pranks' always bellow like cattle. But not me. I suffer in silence.

My wife, Marlies, wouldn't believe me when I told her.

'Go on then,' I said. 'Try me. Press the burning end of your cigarette into my arm.'

Marlies bravely held her cigarette between her fingers. There was soon a smell of singed hair and flesh. I didn't bat an eyelid or move my arm – except to catch Marlies as she fainted.

I want to be like Rocky. Not a weakling. I know that I must win the struggle to keep my knees working. Keeping fit is a constant battle. The thought of a long holiday is a source of great anxiety to me. I'm afraid that if I stop training for any length of time my muscles and ligaments will seize up. Perhaps I'll start falling apart. So, I prefer to continue training, even during the holidays. Twice daily. The rest of the time I enjoy my holiday, spending time with the kids, relaxing with Marlies, joking with my parents and friends. But somewhere at the back of my mind there's always the fear that I might develop a taste for the joys of idleness.

When Marlies says: 'Listen, are you crazy? We're on holiday. So take a rest for three weeks and don't do anything!'

My reply is always the same: 'Darling, that's just not on. I can't allow myself to do that, in my position. Just imagine if I started to enjoy being on holiday so much that I had no desire to get back to the grindstone.'

Mental problems are a lot worse to cope with than dodgy knees. You can see a cut or a broken bone, but you can't see the mental injury. You can sense it deep inside you, somewhere in your body that you can't pin down. It can drive you mad.

After the World Cup, in August and September 1986, I was feeling really low. My nerves felt as though they were being sandpapered. I blamed myself for letting the ball get past me in the final against Argentina and allowing them to get a 1–0 lead. In the end I took two weeks off, but I couldn't leave Cologne because the children had to go to school. After three days at home I'd had more than enough of watching Marlies washing the dishes, doing the ironing and cleaning the house. I went and nosed around the training ground. I had a compulsion to be doing something – perhaps it was a fear of being left alone with my Mexico defeat.

Kessler, the coach, tapped his forehead as though I was mad: 'Go away, you're a bundle of nerves. Any training for you is out of the question. Give yourself a break, get some rest, don't do anything. And stop playing silly buggers!'

Back to dreary idleness. I prowled round the house like a caged lion, getting in Marlies' way the whole time. I'd played in over seventy international matches, and the European and World championships. After six years without a holiday I was completely overwound. I simply couldn't switch off. I'd earned a lot of money. And recognition too. I had a loving wife and two healthy children. And here I was behaving like a certifiable lunatic, afraid of losing my resilience and becoming weak and flabby. Worse still, I caught myself missing my usual holiday in hospital. It was perverse.

Where would my dread of daily routine lead me? Marlies can't imagine how I would survive a day without my 'beloved straightjacket' – football.

'You've got it all wrong,' I protest weakly. 'I dream of living in a farmhouse in the middle of the country. Where there's peace and absolute quiet. No stress. None of the aggravation or obligations I've had to put up with until now in order to create a place for us in the sun. I dream of a completely quiet happy life.'

Marlies is not only beautiful, she's also clever. She simply laughs at these daydreams of mine. And she doesn't say anything. She knows perfectly well that I'm deceiving myself yet again.

The compulsion to succeed not only causes a footballer stress but can also bring him pleasure. He thrills the crowd and thrills with the crowd. Success. Applause. Deep emotions that are not easily replaced. Football is an addiction that devours you and always challenges you to reach greater heights.

I had one objective. I've achieved it and now here I am, up where the air is thinner. And I'm still not content. That's life. Once you've climbed the mountain, the peak seems disappointingly ordinary. All the pleasure lies in the ascent. The joy is anticipatory. After you've reached the top, a feeling of sadness sets in at the thought of having to make the descent or climb the next mountain – a higher and more difficult peak?

Is this a sign of arrogance?

My mother worries about me: 'People like you are never satisfied.' As in the past, she puts her finger on the self-destructive side of my ambition.

The truth is that I'm not afraid of death. The Grim Reaper leaves me completely cold. It can only be better on the other side than it is in the here and now . . .

There are no problems there. Only happiness and tranquillity. And one day we'll all be together again in the hereafter. I'm absolutely convinced of it. The good and the bad will be given one last chance to earn themselves a place among the Chosen. When I cease to enjoy life, and it all becomes too much of a trial, then I wish for peace. The peace that death brings.

In September 1986 after the World Cup, I felt a bit like this: indecisive in goal, panicked by crosses. I trained to excess in order to dispel my anxiety. It was no use. I felt more like retiring behind my net than standing in front of it. From a purely psychological point of view, I was constantly on the defensive. And very depressed.

The newspaper headlines read: 'What's wrong with our national goalkeeper?'; 'Schumacher's mistake' and so on. At a game in Munich, there were morons chanting: 'It's Schumacher's fault we lost the final.'

What could I do? It seemed that only death could put an end to my state of depression and bring me the peace I longed for. I wanted to escape the inhuman demands people made on me, as well as my own goading ambition.

Life can be hell. Is death a quiet refuge?

'Stop it!' said Marlies and Rüdiger when I pondered on these matters out loud. 'You're going to drive yourself crazy – and us too, for that matter.'

But what do they know about my fear of failure? Or about the burden of success? Thank God that I have them both. My children and my family. Otherwise, I would fall even more frequently into the jaws of that wolf, depression.

'Come off the line,' Rolf Herings insisted. 'You've got a mental block about it. Crosses have never been a problem for you before. Be aggressive. The final in Mexico? Forget it! Battiston? Forget that too!'

Between August and October 1986 there were weeks, months, when I lost all self-confidence.

'You left it too late there, Toni! The next one! Well done! Another step to the left! Punch it!' shouted Rolf.

Then: 'Running is always better than jumping. Try and catch the ball. But the best thing is to punch it. Just punch it.'

My coach was treating me like a convalescent. But that's just what I was.

One Monday in October, months after I made that stupid leap into the air in the Aztec Stadium in Mexico, something just clicked inside me. I had recovered my desire to go after the ball.

'That's it! You're not hanging back any more,' said Herings, absolutely delighted. 'At last you're the same old Toni again!'

I was cured of the Mexico syndrome. The ball was my prey again, and I was the tiger. And along with my rediscovered confidence on the field came a new zest for life.

But the moment of truth had yet to come. When? Rolf Herings was waiting, ever patient.

It was the thirteenth day of play into the season, the sky was overcast, it was cold and drizzly – the worst day of the Bundeslige season so far, and the smallest gate as well.

Rüdiger Vollborn, aged twenty-three, the keeper for Bayer Leverkusen, again performs very well against Berlin. The press are already talking of his getting a cap.

'There's no hurry,' says the man himself. He's got plenty of time, he's still young. And then he adds: 'But today's good keepers are already pretty old.'

Admittedly, on that 10 November 1986, I was indeed the old Toni – but not in the sense that Vollborn intended. I was cured. My inhibitions had disappeared. I was back on form.

'Some of the saves Schumacher managed to make were quite incredible,' said Höher, the coach from Nuremberg, the team we were playing against that day.

My inner reflexes were immediately transmitted to my muscles, so that I acted on them correctly at the very last hundredth of a second. I was as quick on the ball as I had ever been. My team-mates and coach were delighted. We won 3–1.

The next day the newspaper *Bild* had put me back at the top of their league table of players for my world-class performance.

'It's all thanks to you, Toni,' said most of the rest of the team enthusiastically.

These compliments were music to my ears. After weeks of despair, of a yawning chasm deep inside me, after anxious glimpses into an unknown future, I was suddenly back on top, where you see things in a new perspective.

'Even Schumacher, our national goalkeeper who's come in for a lot of criticism recently, played with his former excellence,' the *Welt am Sonntag* informed its readers.

Rüdiger Vollborn will have to wait a while longer. I hope he's a patient man.

9

A CAMEL WITH THE
HEART OF A LION

FRANZ BECKENBAUER is in my book the most brilliant footballer since the war. As the national coach, he now has to work with people who are a lot less single-minded about football than he is and a lot less talented. So he gets into a rage, or falls into a state of despair. In Mexico he saw players treat the ball as though it was a hostile foreign body. Franz, who was himself an absolute genius on the field, hasn't yet got used to the idea that he hasn't got a single player of his calibre in the national side.

He once told me perplexedly: 'If I stuck to my guns, we'd be left with only five players. But there are times when you have to come to terms with reality.'

His heartfelt outburst in Mexico – when he said: 'We'll never become world champions with this team' – has to be seen in the light of this.

'You have to take us as we are,' I told him. 'Without great technical skills and not properly trained. We also have to make the best of it.'

This didn't go down very well with Franz. My directness, my fighting spirit and my perfectionism don't always find favour with him. He's of the opinion that I'm over-endowed with these 'qualities'.

'The best is no friend of the good,' as the proverb says. Franz must have heard that somewhere.

But in terms of football, we make an ideal combination: Franz is the embodiment of Brazilian-style, French-style football, whilst I represent the German style. It's a good mixture.

I admire a footballer who's a fighter more than I do the technically skilled player. The wizards with the ball often forget about winning. When their team is losing 2–0, they're already thinking of themselves as 4–0 down. But the fighter says to himself: '2–0, let's take it as 1–0. We only need to get one goal and we're out of trouble. From 2–1 we'll easily catch up!'

A fighting spirit, the will to win – these have become almost dirty words.

'The Germans are only good for running,' people say about us.

So what? I'm always flattered when I hear this. I grew up with this style of football. Running! Throwing yourself into the game! We're certainly less gifted than the Brazilians or the French from the point of view of elegance and feeling, deftness and artistry. But we have a lot more will-power.

I stand by our German style of play and the fight we put into the game. Never giving ground, defending every square centimetre of the field. In World Cup competitions, the highly talented Italians, Brazilians and French have often had to go home early. They play fantastic football, but they don't win. The Brazilians used to have both fighters and artists, but today they only have artists. Wonderful artists. But eleven artists are not enough to win the game. A modern team must have both: a few football geniuses and a lot of solid artisans.

The ideal team – i.e. an unbeatable team – would be a combination of French skill and brilliance, and German robustness and spirit.

At the start of the World Cup series, the Russians demonstrated all these qualities. They ran a lot, and were clever with the ball, with enormous commitment to the game. They were superb. They led 2–0, then 3–0, and not content with that went on to 4–0, 5–0, 6–0. They completely exhausted themselves; they were the victims of their own enthusiasm.

We did the same thing. In the final, we were trailing 2–0. Then we came back 2–1. Jubilation. Finally we made it 2–2. More jubilation and ecstatic rejoicing. We went on playing in the same state of drunken joy, absolutely determined to beat the Argentinians with a decisive third goal in the remaining seven minutes. We had the heart, the fighting spirit, and the form to do it. What was lacking was a cool head capable of thinking tactically.

Franz was the essence of football artistry. He played to win, but also to be watched – fantastic, wonderful football. He puts me in mind of a sculptor who normally produces delicate figurines and then finds himself face to face with novices who have always worked the wood with an axe instead of a carving knife.

He still hasn't come to terms with this.

There's no sign of players like Overath, or footballers with the technique of Flohe, Netzer or Grabowski. German football has yet to find another constellation of star players. Franz has not been able to work miracles. When Jupp Derwall retired and Franz Beckenbauer took his place as chief of the national selection board, I was the only person who remained sceptical: 'I hope to God that people don't think that simply because of Beckenbauer the Germans are going to start playing better football.'

Franz was offended and took this personally. Today he admits I was right.

It's all very well playing beautifully, but is it still feasible these days? The game has got much faster. The strikers have less time to get the ball and make it work for them, less time to show off their skills.

There was an exhibition match at Kaiserlautern in which FC Kaiserlautern's senior team took on their predecessors. The young players attacked Overath mercilessly. The former international ran over to the coaches' bench and shouted: 'Hey, tell the lads to ease up a bit. We want to play some good football!'

It doesn't suit an artist to be disturbed while he's trying to set something up and have his fancy footwork interrupted.

Platini, Tigana, Giresse, Maradona would find it extremely hard to shine in the Bundeslige. When we played against Felix Magath, another football artist, our coach kept on telling us: 'Stick with Magath. Just concentrate on Magath. Give him a hard time.'

It's a matter of putting your opponents off their stride, neutralizing their star player, as we do every Sunday in the Bundeslige. This is the strategy we adopted against France. We just couldn't lose.

Naturally these methods don't encourage technical wizardry or football sorcery. A talented young footballer has only to show himself and his opponents are immediately on his heels. The coach will set a fighter on the artist and the artist is soon 'dead'. Every talented player soon meets his 'killer'.

Our neighbours, the Belgians and the Dutch, are always ready to risk playing offside. This is how they excelled, whereas we made a name for ourselves with our combativeness. That's what we were trained for, day in, day out. It's worth noting that the coach who trains our national youth side, Berti Vogts, was once a 'killer' himself, a fighter, a saboteur. He's played in over ninety internationals.

'Berti Vogts has certainly never played good football,' is what people say, 'but he delivers the goods. So his style of play can't be that bad. It stands to reason.'

This style of play has twice made us world champions. So we can't be getting it all that wrong either.

I have an overdeveloped will to win. Success is my primary objective. Like most football spectators I also appreciate both spontaneity and accurate play. But it's difficult to achieve a balance between two. How is a player to be at once inspired and energetic, intuitive and analytical?

The film director Steven Spielberg has pinned down the same dilemma in his own field:

'I've noticed,' he explains, 'that when I'm making a film, I'm guided by an unknown force. There's nothing mysterious about it, though. Anyone who has ever created something that he's put his heart into has experienced this force. You have to put your trust in it, and not ask any questions. This is the way most of my films are made. The older I get and the more I think about things, the less childlike I feel, and the weaker grows this voice that I've been able to rely on for years.'

It is just the same for footballers. Losing your innocence also means losing your creativity. Once sterility sets in, more of the same kind of training sessions are no help any more. The solution is a balancing act: you have to work like a man possessed to master the technical skills and to develop your strength. Only then can you play with the freshness and recklessness that children possess.

There have been a lot of changes for goalkeepers as well.
A lot more is expected of a keeper than before. As I've
already said, Sepp Maier is my hero. As a young player, I
was dazzled by his style and fascinated by his enthusiasm
and dedication to the game. With all due respect, naturally, I was always saying to myself: 'If that old crock can
carry on playing with a broken finger, then you can do the
same when you're only twenty-five.'

He was thirty-three at the time. Broken finger, broken
nose, sores on his leg – but the game must go on. Pain is a
figment of the imagination. Sepp Maier played four hundred matches in a row, with or without injury, whether it
was raining, snowing, or a mud-bath. He was the arche-
typal professional. It's difficult to compare our styles of
play – though some people say Maier is better at defending
against crosses than I am. In his time, the ball was played
differently, the crosses were slower and came from a
greater distance. There was more time to come off the line
and catch them. Today there's more strength and power
behind the ball. There's practically no way of stopping it
because a striker's cross is like a free kick – it's aimed
straight for the net, with a lot of power packed into it, and
it has a kind of topspin. Perverse!

For this reason, I find any comparison of myself and
Maier unsatisfactory. Too many things have changed, a
lot of things are faster now. And Sepp Maier played with a
world-class side – Beckenbauer, Breitner, Müller, Sch-
warzenbeck. And it shouldn't be forgotten that he had a
strong defence to rely on. But there is one thing we have in
common: we don't go in for acrobatics – except to stop a
ball. Otherwise it's all show – à la Heinze, Nigbur or
Burdenski. But nor am I as totally cool, calm and collected as the Italian goalkeeper Dino Zoff. My maxim is:

stop the ball. And I'll use any means to do so – head, legs, arse, back. The ability to play well on the spot and to run fast are very important. What my coach Rolf Herings says is undeniably true: it's always slower to jump and dive than to run. This is why hurdlers always try to get their feet back on the track as quickly as possible. And why downhill skiers try to limit the duration of their jumps and get back onto the piste. I've been operating on this principle for more than twelve years. The aesthetics of the thing are a secondary issue; the quest for beauty of movement belongs to ballet. People used to say of Nijinsky, the legendary 'god of dance': 'He doesn't leap higher than other dancers but he manages to give the impression that he stays longer in the air. His leaps convey to the audience the feeling of contained strength and at the same time of delicacy.'

But unfortunately all this has little to do with football, except when a side is already confident of having won a match. Only then will the keeper allow himself to show off a little, by way of winking at the public.

Every Monday afternoon I train with Rolf Herings. I practise being under pressure and test my own limitations. For an hour and a half we try out all the most dangerous situations: with the ball coming to the centre of the goal, to the left, the right, when it falls short of you, when it's lobbed over your head, when there's no bounce in it. There are fans present. They enjoy watching me dive across the goal but hardly react at all when I manage to stop a really difficult ball with my foot.

Paradoxically, the best saves are mostly those that follow from an initial error of judgement. A ball aimed at one of the top corners of the net is almost unreachable. Only if I'm in the wrong place, standing near the corner that it's aimed at, would I catch a ball like that. 'Toni's done it again – stopped an unstoppable ball!' say the fans. Little do they know!

But the opposite is equally true. I'm accused of making mistakes that aren't mistakes at all. For instance, in Munich, in September 1986: one of the Bayern players took a corner. Hans-Peter Lehnhoff should have been marking his opponent and wasn't – he even jumped aside, letting the ball past him. I knew that I had practically no chance but I wanted to try and make things difficult for the Bayern striker who was lining himself up to head the ball into the net. I ran at him. No use. And then I'm the one who's blamed for it. Even Beckenbauer thinks it was my fault he scored.

Rolf Herings is one of the rare people whose criticism I'm prepared to take seriously and freely accept. Every Monday afternoon he begins by criticising Saturday's game. Then we both try and correct the mistakes through an appropriate series of reflex exercises. Rolf knows how to deal with me. He doesn't keep rubbing my nose in my weaknesses, but rather tries to develop my strengths. These include the power and accuracy of my throws. Under Rolf's close supervision, I try to throw the ball sixty metres to reach targets that are supposed to represent my team-mates. I do this over and over again until my arms ache and I start seeing black in front of my eyes.

Another intensive and specific exercise: the keeper–striker tackle. We do it again and again, a thousand times, ten thousand times – with the help of mathematical calculations. It isn't very difficult to work out the possibilities of deflecting a long or short corner, or how to make sure the striker doesn't have enough room for manoeuvre. Together we've simulated hundreds of different possibilities and scenarios. First on the drawing board, then on the field. Until I was taking up the appropriate positions in goal as a matter of reflex action. Obviously there's no time for mathematical calculations when you're actually playing. Thought becomes pure reflex – but only after years of working yourself extremely hard.

This is what characterizes my game: being in the right position to deflect the opponent's ball and block his shot at goal. I stay in my area and defend my territory to the last, if necessary by diving headfirst into the legs of an assailant. Real kamikaze stuff.

The memory of that narrow room I slept in as a child also has a big influence on me; I now get claustrophobic. I need air, and space; I'm always having to come off the line out onto the pitch. I even venture as far as the half-way line, terrified of the goal posts falling on my head, or of becoming entangled in the net. As the most isolated of the eleven players, I seek contact with my friends, join them in their attack on the other side, and then immediately have to rush back into position again. I'm at once spectator, player and keeper, and sometimes even director as well. As a spectator in front of the net, the moments of waiting can seem very long.

'You must stay on the line,' I was always being told when I first joined the national side. My team-mates and Derwall, the coach, quickly learned that this was contrary to my nature. And they came to accept what had been axiomatic as far as my previous coach, Rinus Michels, was concerned: the distance between a keeper and his libero must remain constant. This is absolutely correct. The opponent is only really dangerous when he attacks, when he approaches the 30-metre line. Why should there have to be a distance of sixty metres between the keeper and the libero when my own team is attacking? No one's going to score a goal in my net from the half-way line. I need the freedom to go forward, especially as captain of the team. And I shall continue to exercise this freedom in the future.

I've also practised punching the ball, a hundred thousand times, in every conceivable circumstance, until I could punch it to the half-way line and get my team out of any difficult situations.

Throwing and punching rely on intensive weight-training exercises for the upper arms and shoulder muscles, which I've done. I used to be the same shape as a Coca Cola bottle – just as thin. Today I'm an athlete of fairly rugged build. Of course, my thigh muscles aren't as developed as Rummenigge's; but with all the running round the field he has to do, he needs them more than I do in goal.

There's one handicap I've suffered since birth: I'm hopelessly knock-kneed. My joints are consequently weak compared with those in a perfectly normal body. As I've already said, Professor Schneider has prescribed some corrective exercises for this problem, and Rolf Herings helps me with them. Medically speaking, I'm something of a miracle. Without this muscle training I would not be able to go on playing and I almost certainly would never have been able to survive 75 international matches in succession. Generally speaking, I try to shield my knees from knocks and fractures by building up a layer of protective muscle.

It's also very important to intimidate the strikers on the opposing side. They must think: 'Careful now, I'm approaching the net and that's no will-'o-the-wisp standing in front of it but a burly goalkeeper. A dragon in front of his cave, a devil of a jack-in-the-box.'

The penalty area is my territory, with the goal at the heart of it. And I have to guard this sanctuary – this is something the opposing strikers must be made aware of.

Simply on the basis of what he sees, a player is less frightened of a small goalkeeper. So you have to command respect by bringing every means at your disposal into play: your muscles, a show of aggression, a brutal look in your eye. The striker must get worried. Ronnie Borchers of Waldhof Mannheim sees it this way: 'When you enter Toni's penalty area, the goal always seems to get smaller, you don't really think you've got a chance and you start thinking about saving your own neck.'

That's the way it should be. And that's why I train so hard. Only no amount of training can rectify my knock-knees. I have to admit that I've often suffered on account of their ungainliness. A goalkeeper with long legs and knock-knees looks absurd, I used to think. But they have since become my hallmark: knock-knees = Schumacher, and that's that.

Unfortunately football, albeit a substitute for actual conflict, fairly frequently degenerates into genuine psychological warfare. Your aim is to try and intimidate the opponent by projecting an impression of yourself on him so that he hardly dares approach the ball. Dirty looks, snarls, obscene gestures, coarse insults – the spectators don't notice most of what happens on the pitch. The players can therefore be quite crude and brutal towards each other. Blind anger and spite, the worst aspects of human nature, are given free rein.

Various parts of the anatomy naturally form the largest category of insults: the word 'arsehole' is usually embellished by some choice adjective. But there's worse. I start seeing red when I get called some of the crudest names. I've heard them all, and to be honest, I'm not entirely blameless in this respect myself. My opponents and teammates have heard me effing and blinding with the best of them. I have my own favourite expressions, and I've even sworn at the referee occasionally when I'm angry . . . but not so loudly that anyone could hear me. Uli Stein, for a long time the number two keeper, would openly accuse a referee who he thought was not being evenhanded of taking bribes. I've never gone that far; as captain of the national side I have to exercise some self-control and not set a bad example to the younger players in the team.

Jostling your opponents and insulting them is both a reaction to the pressure you yourself are under and a way of trying to throw your opponent off balance. The verbal abuse is designed to interefere with his ability to concentrate – even if only for a very brief moment.

But by far and away the worst thing that can happen to you is to get spat at.

Anyone who has ever been spat at will understand why there are crimes of passion. For the first few seconds it's as though you're paralysed. You tremble with rage and loathing. Your blood starts to boil. Hatred stirs within you and for a moment you can't breathe. There is nothing worse. Football ceases to be a substitute for war and becomes the real thing; the knives are out . . . It takes you hours, days, to get over the dreadful injury to your self-esteem, to be able to calm down.

It's hard for referees. They have to take criticism from all sides. They can't swear back at anyone – but they get their revenge. This usually takes the form of a decision in the course of the game.

It's not easy for the man in black to withstand pressure from the crowd and the coaches' bench. Bundeslige coaches – such as Uerdingen's Karl-Heinz Feldcamp – have their own cunning ways of getting at him: they manage to heighten the tension by gesturing and whistling, by turning and appealing to the crowd. With the crowd's support, pressure is brought to bear on the referee. The clever refs ignore the whistling and the verbal abuse from the players. The really clever ones react in the same way as the proverbial monkeys: they hear nothing, see nothing, say nothing. But other refs tear up and down the field like a wounded boar, with the players and crowd teasing and tormenting the poor man's nerves until he cracks. Overath and Breitner were notorious for this. They could wear a referee down by always shouting a bit louder, always crowding him a bit more – many's the referee who's been tamed in this way.

Being a referee gives you authority over twenty-two players – or does it? The fact that a person chooses to become a referee is no guarantee that he's got the right character for the job. Some refs use their position to work off the frustration they've been building up all week by being dictatorial and autocratic at the weekend. After all, the referee's decision is always final.

And many of them seem to take revenge on the good players for the fact that they themselves have never become stars, for it's often failed football stars who are chosen to preside over a whole cast of stars for ninety minutes. At the weekend the man in black becomes a different person: the whistle blows and then it's watch out anyone who doesn't do as he's told or tries to argue the toss. He'll just get shown the yellow card, or even occasionally the red card. Disputing the referee's decision only makes things worse.

On the pitch, the referee is all-powerful. When I go into a game, I try to see him as impartial and objective. I don't see the man in black as an opponent – though he becomes one if he starts favouring the other side in the course of play. But if he's on our side, then of course he'll get my approval: 'Excellent decision. Well done – fantastic!' And in this way I try to encourage his sympathy for us and for our game.

On the other hand, if I consider he's being unfair, and

that he's responding to the pressure of a hostile crowd, then he becomes the twelfth man we're playing against on the field. Perhaps even then it would be better to praise his decisions, in the hope of winning him over. But sometimes it's simply beyond my capability to restrain myself and I just tell him what I think of him, no holds barred . . .

The supposedly impartial referee is not someone I consider basically as an enemy. Sometimes his decisions baffle me, but his responsibilities defy all reason. Modern football has become such a fast game, the players are more insolent, the crowds less civilised – and the television cameras are always there, watching the game in close-up.

The kind of football being played today is simply too much for a single referee to cope with.

The example we should follow is that of ice-hockey, a game that's so fast it takes three referees to umpire a match and supervize what happens on the ice. Two would be enough for football. One who would always be watching the ball – he would rule on the free kicks, corners and penalties; while the other would follow the game from a distance, taking a global view of the match. The important decisions would of course be taken by both refs. The linesmen would in future continue to monitor the boundaries and be consulted on off-side decisions; they would be excluded from any other type of decision.

And finally, professional footballers deserve professional referees. There ought to be professional referees for Bundeslige matches – and of course at international level. The decisions made by the man in black are too important to be left to amateurs. A referee's whistle can make the difference between winning and losing, with millions of marks at stake, for a whole team or club. The best qualified people for this job are former professional footballers: they're wise to everything that goes on – after all, you can't teach an old monkey new tricks.

Referees ought to be better paid. For a league match they should get 3,000 marks, not 200–300. Their fee for an international ought to be 5,000 marks. And finally, they should pay their own way and meet the expense of their own board and lodging. In the European Cup there's a rival competition going on: which team is giving the referee the best perks? Four-star hotels and the most exclusive restaurants are barely enough for a referee, provisions are made so that he doesn't lack for company . . . The contest can vary: which referee will go home with most money in his pocket? This is what the clubs are doing. Cologne is perhaps an exception: the referees there are still treated as amateurs.

A person who's well paid for his job is better able to resist bribery. The number of aberrant referees' decisions would undoubtedly drop if their fees were increased. Professionalism is the best protection against misconduct and arbitrary decisions. It's not only the players who must strive to rise above amateurism. The same goes for referees, coaches, managers and members of the boards of directors.

10

THE NATIONAL SIDE

Ask a group of bureaucrats to design a tank and what they'll come up with is a camel.

This saying could be applied very well to the way the German Football Federation (the DFB) operates. All administrations have a tendency to become an end in themselves. Fortunately, the President of the DFB, Hermann Neuberger, is in control. His leadership acts as a counterbalance to the dead-weight of a system responsible for nearly forty Bundeslige clubs and four million amateur players. In the long term, it's virtually impossible for the same authority to try and deal with such divergent interests as those of the national team, of professional footballers, of the First and Second Division Bundeslige clubs, and of the amateur clubs. The amateurs are a burden to the profession. And conversely, the greater influence that the Bundeslige clubs have over the DFB is a cause of annoyance and frustration to the amateurs. A separation of the two is desirable, and consideration of a new efficient system of management is called for.

Let's be bold: there could still be a self-governing DFB, but in future there should be two separate boards of management – one to deal with professional football, the other for the amateur game. Hermann Neuberger would continue as head of the professional board. Franz Beckenbauer would become his general manager, a kind of chief executive who would have various experts to deal with finance, publicity, training, etc.

I would like to see Mr Mayer-Vorfelder, the extremely ambitious chairman of the Bundeslige Committee and Minister of Culture for Baden-Württemberg, chairing the amateur board. The job would give him a genuine opportunity to show that the Football Federation doesn't have to be run as a kind of banana republic. Paul Breitner would be his general manager, being the ideal candidate for this job! He would at last have a chance to come into his own instead of always complaining . . .

Franz Beckenbauer cannot conceive of such a revolution, so I've heard. But these changes are urgently needed.

If Hermann Neuberger were to leave the DFB for some reason or other, or to retire, we would have to be prepared to see the DFB fall into utter chaos. His presence and autocratic style are the principle reasons why more mistakes haven't been made. But the weight of responsibility will gradually prove too much for him. Far too many trifling matters are referred to him for arbitration. A successor who didn't match up to Neuberger would be completely defeated by this, sooner or later. This is all very flattering to the incumbent president but spells disaster for the DFB.

At present, the team manager Beckenbauer invariably has to consult Neuberger before he does anything at all. In Mexico he and the head of the delegation, Braun, were reporting to him ten times a day. And often about the most insignificant issues. There just isn't enough delegation within the DFB.

One example of this unhealthy lack of delegation was the debate over my selection for the European Championship that took place in Paris in 1984 – two years after my 'foul' on Battiston. The problem was whether my inclusion in the team wasn't taking something of a risk, and whether the French would see it as provocative.

Shortly before the dramatic international in Strasbourg, there had been a match between the two national youth teams in the South of France. The German goalkeeper had been given a very hostile reception by the home crowd. The spectators had shouted: 'Schumacher! Schumacher!' Berti Vogts saw fit to raise the matter at a meeting at which Jupp Derwall was present (perhaps he suddenly saw himself as a Minister of Foreign Affairs?). Our national coach was faced with a dilemma. No one seemed able to take a decision or ask anyone else for advice. I was met with silence, ambivalence and evasiveness – but no clear word. How was I supposed to have any confidence in Derwall after I'd heard about his 'predicament'?

So I telephoned Hermann Neuberger myself.

If the German team had had a general manager, I would have been able to speak to him about it and wouldn't have had to bother the President.

I went to see Neuberger in his office in Frankfurt, and he told me without any beating about the bush: 'As far as I'm concerned, there's only one thing that counts: as a sportsman, your entitlement to a place in the team is indisputable. I'm prepared to put my name to this in writing.'

This attracted some sharp criticism: 'Toni gets a blank cheque' ran the headlines. There was some truth in this.

But the real problem was that Neuberger had to lay himself open to criticism in this way.

How effectively management systems and structures operate – whether in the field of economics, politics or administration – depends on the people who use them and apply them. In other words, even the best organisation in the world can't compensate overnight for a disastrous lack of talent and poor quality of personnel.

The converse is equally true: rational structuring and a clear division of labour will reduce the number of time- and energy-consuming conflicts, and enable a team to improve its performance – whether in industry, politics, scientific research or sport.

There is no convincing reason why the same principles shouldn't be applied to football. And the best place to start would be at the national level. It's about time that here in the land of organisation we stopped being so dilettante, and perhaps even sought advice from businessmen: we must introduce new structures!

This was probably not such an important issue in the past, when we could compensate for a weakness in the management structure with stronger personalities. Thinking back to the glorious postwar period when Germany proved to be a football miracle, that came about as a result of good luck and successful improvization on the part of the legendary Sepp Herberger. I'm too young to be able to talk from experience, but I believe that football in those days didn't require such total dedication and commitment as it does today.

After Sepp Herberger came Helmut Schön, whose greatest contribution was his success in making football a part of everyday life. Schön was an almost unapproachable coach, but with a great deal of intelligence and authority he set about dealing with both the organizational and psychological problems within the national team. And what a team it was! Helmut Schön had the good fortune to have such outstanding players as Franz Beckenbauer, Sepp Maier, Gerd Müller and Wolfgang Overath to work with. It was as though he were the conductor of an orchestra made up of very talented soloists. Even under an undistinguished baton, they would still have played good music.

After the 1974 World Cup, Müller, Overath, Breitner (only temporarily) and Grabowski left the national team. And this unique constellation of talent dispersed. The hope that a similar rapport between coach and players might be re-established still persists, but so far this has failed to materialize.

Jupp Derwall had to put his own team together, and it was a team that remained undefeated after 23 games. They played fantastically good football, mostly against weaker opponents. The euphoria that this unbroken run of victories gave rise to had disastrous consequences. Derwall was celebrated throughout the country, many of the players put him on a par with Helmut Schön. But Derwall was weak, his authority did not go unquestioned. He was simply too decent a chap, too chummy with all the players. He was always after a good friendly atmosphere. He appealed to his players' good sense and never laid down the law with them. I'm sorry, but this just won't wash. It was bound to end in fiasco.

It simply couldn't work: only a very strict coach with a strong personality can afford to allow any familiarity to enter his relations with the team – and even then only on condition that the captain recognizes his authority. This was possible between Schön and Beckenbauer, because they had respect for each other; it was almost a father–son relationship. This was fortuitous and an extremely rare occurrence. The Derwall–Rummenigge partnership that succeeded it was not a happy one. They were too much alike, even in their inability to assert themselves. And both lacked the necessary authority. Breitner, the third man, was too dominant a personality, the instigator of what happened by day at 'Schlucksee' and of those notorious night-time activities in Madrid.

The team today is certainly better than it was then, but somewhat precarious. Despite his qualities – sporting, technical and human – Franz Beckenbauer is more of a brother to us than a figure of authority. Until the 1986 World Cup Karl-Heinz Rummenigge was his captain. And on account of Rummenigge's almost diplomatic reserve and his aversion to conflicts of any kind, Beckenbauer often – and too often needlessly – had to grasp the nettle himself. A better division of responsibility is required and should be put into operation as soon as possible.

The way I see it, a captain of the national side could have an even more important function than the coach. Naturally, this presupposes a completely different set-up: a general manager, such as Franz Beckenbauer, and a less well-known personality but undoubted football expert as coach. The captain would assume some of the responsibilities that have until now fallen on the shoulders of the coach. In this way we would be able to straighten the team out, and re-establish some good old discipline, with the players putting into practice on the pitch the tactics decided on beforehand. I'm quite sure these reforms would be a great success.

The coach would in future be responsible for the form, football technique and training of his team. The players' psychological welfare, any disciplinary measures to be taken against them, any encouragement or censure they were to receive, everything relating to the individual's responsibilities would be dealt with jointly by the captain and the coach. All decisions and problems would ultimately be referred to the general manager, who would act as arbitrator since he would be able to see things from a distance, within an overall context.

In my happiest dreams I see Beckenbauer in the general manager's seat. Franz has other dreams, I believe. He sees Günther Netzer as manager, and Berti Vogts as assistant coach, while he himself would continue as coach. This idea doesn't appear to have the support of the DFB. But even if Franz were successful in getting his reforms implemented they would only solve half the problems.

In the meantime, as captain of the national eleven, I would like to have at least a monthly meeting with our coach-cum-general manager Beckenbauer. I want to be able to liaise between the delegation, the selection chief, the manager and the team. This is only feasible if I'm kept fully informed of what goes on.

The captain has an important role to play, whether at club or national level. He's responsible for the motivation of the rest of the team and shouldn't be so naïve as to swallow everything his team-mates say – as Derwall was. It's puerile to think that just because it's an honour to be selected to represent your country, the players are going to put everything they've got into winning.

In 1982, in Spain, Derwall must have realized – too late – that every man on his ship was doing just as he pleased. Derwall had lost all credibility both with the players and the football officials. He was constantly being called up before the DFB, so that the DFB could tell him exactly what to do the whole time. He allowed himself to be reduced to just a mouthpiece and ceased to be worthy of respect. We liked him, but he was never feared or respected by us. Whether players were undisciplined, lacking in will-power or simply lazy, they had nothing to fear – there was never any penalty to pay. It was the beginning of the end.

Personally, I probably suffered least from the lack of authority. Generally speaking, I don't need a coach. I know what's good for me, and I take charge of my own training, with the help of the coach who works with the goalkeepers. I'm informed of the strategy we're to adopt in a game, and I also have some understanding of the implications, but as keeper I'm only marginally involved. I don't need anyone to supervise me. I've learned to be reasonable about what time to go to bed, what I eat and drink, and when I can afford to amuse myself. But a great many of the younger players need a 'big brother' to make sure they observe some discipline. Not a sergeant-major but a 'captain' who'll make sure they have a guilty conscience about any back-sliding.

The new type of coach ought to be concerned with completely different issues. He cannot and must not take responsibility for absolutely everything. Above all, he ought to be a technical director, in charge of the shape of the team, and of the tactics of the game, and nothing else. The general manager – if I had my way – would have to be of a completely different calibre. He would treat the players as grown men – as they deserve to be – who would like an opportunity for discussion and the chance to air their criticisms. But when there are decisions to be made, then he's the one to make them.

I still think that Franz is the right man for the job. Especially since, in my own personal view, he has learned from his mistakes – those errors of judgement, made both before and during the 1986 World Cup in Mexico, that no one expected of him.

Compared with Jupp Derwall, Franz Beckenbauer had an incredible advantage in his relations with the press, the officials and the players. Everyone knew that he was Germany's great football star. Whatever he said had to be right. People expected him – as the great football personality, as the player with over one hundred international caps to his credit – to have lots of recommendations and constructive criticism to make.

All things considered, none of the important things have escaped his attention. I admit that I've occasionally been delighted by the initiatives he's taken. Didn't he always say: 'You ought never to be too direct in telling the truth, at least not in public.'

For purely organizational reasons, it's not possible to introduce such radical reform before the next European Championship. But why shouldn't the reforms go through in time for the World Cup in 1990? It would be an ideal combination having Neuberger as the President of the DFB and Beckenbauer as General Manager of the national side.

I see Horst Köppel making a very good coach; he's very competent technically, and gets on better with the players, psychologically speaking, than Berti Vogts. It would be down to the captain to make sure relations were good and morale was high.

Before any international match, the team should spend a week together. Everyone would be able to get any feelings of animosity off their chests, and clear the air of any prejudices; any sense of frustration would also be worked off. Everyone would get to know each other better – it's really dreadful how little we get to talk to each other. As things stand, too much responsibility lies with the coach: he has to preside over discussions, train the players and look after their mental well-being. The players ought to be

able to talk amongst themselves, and not just sound off at
each other. By talking, they would gain a better understanding both of themselves and their team-mates. After
all, a training camp is not a meeting place for deaf-mutes.

As far as the Bundeslige goes, it would be good if the
club captains got together twice a year, in order to defuse
any build-up of hostility or aggression between the teams.
The referees, DFB officials, team doctors, the general
manager and coach of the national side, as well as the club
presidents would also be invited to attend, so that they
could explain the problems and difficulties they face. That
way, you could prevent the takeover of the national side
by any 'Mafia'.

Until now coaches have always condoned the way that
players from the same part of the country always sit
together: there's the 'Cologne table', the 'Munich table',
the 'Hamburg table'. It's well known what this leads to –
just remember what happened in Mexico.

I think it would be a good idea to draw lots for places.
Everyone's name would be put into a hat, the captain
would give them all a good shake, and the coach would
draw out five names for each table. That way the table
formations would be completely random: players from
Hamburg would sit next to players from Cologne, and
Munich players next to the so-called 'legionnaires' –
players like Littbarski and Förster who play for foreign
clubs – and there would be no more cliques.

A training camp ought not to be solely concerned with
exercise, running, eating, massage, sleeping and endless
boredom . . .

'Idleness is the root of all evil,' so the proverb goes. It's
true. There has to be some kind of entertainment. The
general managers, coaches, captains and team doctors
will have to rule on this. What forms of entertainment and

amusement are compatible with preparing for the game? The training programme ought to be scheduled to leave the players with time for leisure. When a player is selected for the national side, aren't his form and technical skills taken for granted? Does he really have to start all over again and learn how to stop a ball? The whole point of the training camp is to weld together eleven players drawn from different clubs to produce a national side. Finding out whether one player is better at running and the other better at jumping is something that ought to be done beforehand – by liaising with the club coaches. The function of a training camp is to bring together the best twenty players out of the four hundred professional footballers in the country, and cultivate mental cohesion among them and a shared style of play; to give them a feeling of solidarity. But not just when they get onto the pitch.

This team spirit has nothing to do with sing-songs round a camp-fire. We're not boy scouts any more. Why shouldn't we have a disco one evening (without alcohol), or see a play, or invite speakers to talk on a particular subject – maybe writers, or various kinds of sportsmen? Is it really necessary to be stupefied with boredom for seven weeks just because you're one of the twenty best footballers in Germany?

Why not, for instance, organize a tennis tournament for the footballers, sponsored by one of the big companies, such as Lufthansa or Coca Cola? This would definitely create a good atmosphere. Everyone would play – the twenty-two footballers, four coaches, the doctor and the DFB officials would be divided into six teams. It would be a proper tournament with a prize for the winning team. The journalists could report on the progress of the tournament and stop writing sensational 'exclusives' on friction between the players or scare stories about injuries.

It would also give the players something to talk about and the opportunity for some friendly competition. The players would be getting good exercise fairly painlessly; it wouldn't seem like hard work.

Anyone who can play football well is good with a ball, even a tennis ball. It's not beyond the bounds of possibility that someone like Boris Becker could come and spend the day with the national eleven. Three hours of tennis lessions with Boris would be a great reward for the winners of the tournament!

Other prizes could be a trip to New York or Wimbledon for the tennis tournaments there. Golf wouldn't be a bad idea either – Bernhard Langer could be our guest. And why not a chess tournament with Kasparov? We could have an *à la carte* choice, something to suit each of the twenty-two players. Boredom is the worst of poisons. When it starts to take root, as it did in Mexico, the chances of everyone getting along together harmoniously are pretty hopeless.

A training camp will never be a nest of angels. But showing a minimum of regard and consideration for one another is something we can achieve. It's the tone that makes the music.

11

THE BUNDESLIGE:
AN IDLE BUNCH

THE YOUNGER German players are beginning to get a bit more agile, a bit more lively, and technically better than the older players who've been manning the game so far. But they don't have the know-how and perseverance of their elders. Since Mexico, only one young player has emerged who's got what it takes: Thomas Berthold. His game used to be all over the place. Now he's tightened it up – he cottoned on in time.

Olaf Thon looked very promising until his injury in Mexico. Franz Beckenbauer suggested he stayed on and watched some world-class players from about as close as anyone can get; it would have been a great chance to discover the football giants' secret of success. But Olaf chose to go back home.

Even with the best will in the world, I can't understand that. Nor can Berti Vogts. Twenty years ago Berti went and watched the World Cup in England from the trainers' bench – at his own expense. Just in order to learn, to see players like Bobby Charlton in action, to analyze the techniques and tactics of the game.

So I'll say it again, loud and clear, in black and white: 'Many young players are lazy shirkers! And some of them are also culpably stupid.' Olaf Thon is a prime example.

He came on to me in a right old state: 'So you think I'm a "lazy shirker", do you?'

This young cock-of-the-walk was in the national team and took my original remark to be aimed at him, because it didn't occur to him that I was actually commenting on the Bundeslige.

'If the shoe fits you,' I said, 'then wear it.'

The younger generation of players – and I'm not trying to be dog-in-the-manger about this – has too easy a time of it in the clubs. They only need to show a glimmer of talent and the next thing they're signed up with a contract. Right from the word go, they're coddled and spoiled, getting fifty thousand, sixty thousand, seventy thousand marks a years for the rawest beginner's performance. The result: they've all got their super-video recorders, their fast cars, and so on. The conversation in the showers and changing rooms is real high-society stuff.

'What are we doing today?' asks one. 'Playing tennis or surfing?'

'Oh no, let's paint the town red,' replies the other.

Most of them pay for tennis coaching, golf lessons or riding instructors. Why don't any of them get their own football coach? They could certainly do with one – they need to shoot better, dribble better, pass better.

When I let a goal in, I feel like going beserk. These young gentlemen take it all much more in their stride; they almost seem not to care. They're 'cool'. They have no ambition, no will to win. They play neither good nor bad football; they play without passion.

They settle for mediocrity instead of delivering the

goods. And they'll soon be getting 200,000 marks a year for that! Handed to them on a plate. They think like office workers. A five-hour day. La dolce vita. Mediocrity is the name of the game. It's disgraceful that they get away with it. They have nothing to fear. There's no competition to threaten them.

Ever since I first started playing football, I've always turned up an hour before training begins. Not that anyone forced me to. At Cologne the coach now has to insist that everyone does half an hour's warm-up. Otherwise some of the players would arrive just ten minutes beforehand.

Should club players have to live in? Why not? And the sooner the better. The youth players must be worked much more intensively. They need the best coaches. The whole of school and youth football should not be left in the hands of amateurs.

'In many clubs,' says Beckenbauer, 'it's some old chap in the village, or the vicar, or the publican who trains the kids. They help the kids keep in good physical shape, but they don't know much about football technique. The kids have their fun and run around from morning till night – just like clockwork hares that have been wound up and left to get on with it!'

Ernest Happel, the HSV coach from Hamburg, goes even further in an interview with *Der Spiegel*: 'Apparently there's talk of setting up schools to train footballers. What a joke! A player like Beckenbauer, or Cruyff didn't go to any school to learn football, they learned it in the street. Today everyone's well off. But the best footballers have always emerged when times are hard.'

Happel's right.

Training runs and more training runs – that's all we do these days. Which means not enough time is spent learning to control the ball. We probably regard the human body too much as a machine.

Perhaps this goes back to our German mentality. We did after all build the Volkswagen, the most successful car ever; from an aesthetic point of view, it's a disaster, but it's still the best-selling car in the world. Bolstered by our success, we continue to turn a blind eye to style and design. Ferrari, Maserati, Lamborghini have created some beautiful cars, but as far as quality and durability go, there's never been anything to touch a Mercedes. If you could refine the design of Mercedes, make it more elegant, and give it a touch of Italian class, you'd have the best car in the world. And if someone could take the German football team in hand. . .

Once a style of leadership has proved itself at a national level, then it ought to be applied at club level. My dearest wish is to see much more efficient professional managers running the clubs, and stemming the blight of amateur incompetence. There are already exceptions: Bayern Munich, where Uli Hoeness is manager, and HSV, where Felix Magath is boss. But most club presidents are no more than ambitious conceited bureaucrats who are simply not qualified to run a professional football club or even to sit on the executive board. In Cologne, for instance, President Weiand and his long-standing vice-president come from gambling backgrounds: lotteries and the tote are their business – undoubtedly a very worth-while occupation but, from a professional point of view, one that involves no risk or challenge. Both men are used to success. Lottery money just finds its way into the tills every week, no problem. The only 'challenge' lies in investing the money profitably. So the management of FC Cologne are no daredevils, and the situation is the same in most other clubs. Hardly any of the boards of directors allow the manager of the club a free hand – Munich being an exception. The presidents are very full of themselves, they think they're irreplaceable. In fact, they either have little time for a club or else they don't really know how to run one. The mistakes they make have to be sorted out by others, and the players are the ones who suffer. Naturally. It's the manager, the coach or the players who carry the can. All the usual scapegoats. And the more speed the hiring-firing merry-go-round picks up, the deeper we get stuck into the same rut . . . Have I made myself clear enough?

In Cologne, for instance, there are some very competent people, from the worlds of finance and politics, sitting on the board. But their functions do not allow them any real participation in the management of the club, which has a budget of fifteen million marks a year. The power lies entirely in the hands of the President. The managers simply carry out directives. Advertising contracts and sponsorship deals pile up and are regarded as proof of financial success. This is complete nonsense. It would be much better to have a good team. That's the sign of a good manager. A good team plays enjoyable football. This is what fills stadiums and puts money in the till. Here again, Uli Hoeness is an interesting example. Admittedly, he's lucky in that he faces no competition from any other club within a 200 km radius. Nuremberg and Stuttgart are pretty far away. Here in the Rhineland and in the Ruhr the situation is different: there's Bochum, Schalke, Düsseldorf, Leverkusen, Uerdingen, Cologne, Dortmund, Gladbach . . . A spectator could – theoretically speaking – drop into eight different stadiums within the space of ninety minutes. And for that reason the need for reform seems all the more urgent; drastic action is called for.

I propose a five-point programme:

1. The recruitment of top managers from the business sector as directors on the club boards.

2. The appointment by the boards of a general manager, who's to be given a completely free hand. He would have to give an account of himself every year.

3. The general manager would earn a lot of money. He would be responsible for the acquisition and transfer of players, coaches, and doctors.

4. The coach could be a complete nobody, perhaps even a newly qualified Physical Education instructor. In the new club structure, the coach would occupy a background position, while the general manager would have to answer for bad investments, bad management, any deficits, mistakes, and poor judgement in the buying of players.

5. It would also be the general manager's job to keep tabs on the coach, insist on results, and organize a systematic training programme.

The training programme would specify what was to be done in the week, the month, the year. The coach would have to update regularly the strikers' times for 100 metres. The general manager would insist that players improved their performance – on the basis of a day's work consisting of training from eight till five. A war on laziness – a disease that's widespread in the Bundeslige – would be declared.

There's no point in making goalkeepers run. It achieves nothing. More gymnastics are what's needed. A thirty-year-old defence player ought to be able to run 100 metres in 12 seconds. A 22-year-old striker should cover the distance 4/10ths of a second faster. With training, there's no reason they shouldn't.

This is how I imagine the ideal general manager of a club: very hard-working, at the club from eight in the morning till six in the evening, always available. He has the authority, but he isn't authoritarian. He's an expert on football technique and also has good business sense. He's particularly interested in the youth players. He puts his best coaches on to them, nothing is spared where they are concerned. After all, the next generation of players has to be trained. Why shouldn't he cultivate his own elite, instead of paying astronomical fees at the beginning of each season for young players from other clubs?

In this way I would like to encourage former professional footballers to apply themselves more than they have done until now to rooting out young talent. There's talent just waiting to be spotted in various competitions and youth games throughout the country. Our pool of young talent is much bigger than generally assumed. This talent must be trained *before* it comes into professional football. For our young players, only the best is anywhere near good enough – that means the best coaches, as long as they're convinced of the truth of this argument and of the importance of their task.

Which club will be the first to attempt this? I know just the man for the job at Cologne: the former international player Heinz Flohe. He's great on technique and would be able to communicate his enthusiasm to young players, and instil in them application, skill, tactical ability and the tricks of the trade – in other words, all the finesse of the really good footballer.

As for the professionals, I envisage a complete retraining programme. People may think I'm obsessed with the subject, but I firmly believe that any reform must extend to the technical and physical training of players. Most important is to work the reflexes and help the player reach a level of technical skill that will enable him to cope with all the different kinds of situation that might arise in an actual game.

And I would also put a stop to everyone having to do the same training. What's the point of making twenty-two players perform the same exercises at the same time? No coach can supervize them all properly. I've worked out my own training schedule, which allows for the footballer's training to be personalized:

7.45:   Special training for two strikers and two backs, with fifteen minutes gym, stretching exercises, etc.

8.00:   Tackling, under a coach's supervision; player against player, defender against striker, left wing against right back, etc. For the strikers this involves trying to keep the ball, outwitting their opponent, and dribbling with the ball. The defenders on the other hand have to try and get the ball off their opponent without fouling them. This could work miracles!

8.45:   Second training group: libero and centre-half begin their gym drill at the same time as three other strikers and a goalkeeper.

9.00:   The first training group makes way for the second. One striker kicks crosses from left, right, all directions. The two defenders try to stop the other two strikers from getting to the ball and shooting at the goal. This goes on for one hour.

9.45: The next group: midfield players. Training for accuracy and precision in passes: they have to kick the ball – accurately – to a partner standing thirty metres away. Dummies could be used to practise with. This would undoubtedly lead to a drop in the number of bad passes. This exercise should be repeated a thousand times over, until the player can find the dummy at thirty metres, forty metres, fifty metres . . . With forty-five minutes spent on each distance.

In this way all the players get some special training before midday. There will be masseurs on hand. Some players will be taking a shower while others are warming up; the doctors will be available for consultation and anyone who wants to speak to the manager will be able to do so during the breaks.

11.00: After some exercises, the three keepers and strikers spend an hour practising penalty kicks.

12.00: Break until 1.45.

The afternoon programme is also organised in small groups. Players who specialize in heading the ball, practice heading crosses into the net. Dribblers run with the ball through a 100-metre slalom course with irregularly staked obstacles; greater ball-control or intensive physical training will enable players to improve their times on this run. Unlike football or other team sports, there can be no dispute over the standard of individual performances in athletics. The stop-watch cannot lie. A time of 10.4 seconds for 100 metres is better than 11 seconds. There are no two ways about it. It's more difficult to measure the quality of a striker. But his speed and success at getting the ball into the net can indeed be measured. I would put up on a blackboard in the club, for all to see, the times achieved by our forward line for 100 metres in the course of training.

The day ends with a practice game in which all the club players take part. A new method of training, but does this not also mean a new generation of coaches? Are old hands like Lattek, Happel, Feldcamp and Co going to be on the spot from morning till evening, as my proposal entails?

Perhaps they'll tell me that I urgently need to see a psychiatrist when they read my proposals. I can see their point. Why should anyone work hard all day when they can earn their 30,000 marks a month with the minimum of effort?

In the world of football there's no such thing as an eight-hour day. Having to be at your place of work isn't an issue. Most people operate on the principle: 'If no one calls you, don't show up.'

Certainly on an international level, German football has been relatively successful. Does this mean we've been getting it right so far?

Certainly not. We've acquitted ourselves not too badly because discipline and determination have been our unbeatable strong suits. But we must overcome our technical weakness and our defective skill with ingenuity and intuition. Then we'd have an excellent chance of making German football the best in the world and of making sure that it stayed that way.

One thing is certain: if my hopes are ever realized and I become president or general manager of a club, then the coaches would have to fall in with my views on the work ethic and the amount of time they have to put in. No successful businessman or politician or freelancer works less than fifty to sixty hours a week. These are the people we should take as our yardstick.

And my forward planning would extend to over a year: important dates – such as matches, training sessions, or holidays – would be scheduled a long time in advance.

On Friday evenings the assistant coach would have to go and watch our opponents play – and I mean that he should go himself and not send someone in his place. My kind of coach does not spend the weekend in front of the box, and he doesn't get sozzled. My kind of coach isn't faced with the problem of having to kill time.

If you go into a game this well prepared, you can lose once in a while with a clear conscience.

The performance we get from the coaches on the sideline is quite unnecessary. What's the point of all that absurd yelling and shouting and gesticulating? What's needed is a cool-headed, unflappable coach who gives clear instructions.

The serious work can begin when Schlappner, of Waldhof Mannheim, finally stops ranting and raving and his chequered hat finally disappears from the cameramen's viewfinder.

Even the overexcitable Rehhagel, of Werder Bremen, has calmed down and is performing better. Could this have anything to do with the club's lack of success? Coaches are always jumping up and down when their team wins; when they lose, they cower dejectedly on their benches, like little heaps of misery.

This was not true of Georg Kessler, at the end of his time with Cologne, before he got the sack in September 1986.

For me Kessler had many of the qualities of a good coach. He was always there before me, long before training was due to start. He was hard-working, he could plan ahead and co-ordinate players' activities. His professional judgement wasn't always beyond criticism, but he

compensated for the weaknesses in his tactical understanding of the game by his considerable knowledge of
training methods. He wasn't a particularly good teacher
and was unable to communicate his ideas to the players;
his ideas and objectives weren't always easy to grasp.
Perhaps he was too intelligent, too distinguished, and too
polite. Perhaps he lacked the necessary degree of brutality
in his dealings with the players. But he also foundered on
the poor physical form of some of the players – Toni
Schumacher among them. Kessler shouldn't have been
blamed for this.

Klaus Allofs was another of the players who went
through a bad patch. He didn't score a single goal under
Kessler. This was very embarrassing for him, particularly
as he became an ace goal-scorer again after Kessler's
departure as scapegoat – until he was injured.

When he left, Kessler didn't utter a single unpleasant or
angry word. He accepted the loss of his job without a
murmur. He was well aware that the coach occupies the
most vulnerable position in a club. He is the cut-out
device in an obsolete system whose structures of responsibility are completely ossified.

The years Hennes Weisweiler was at Cologne are for
me unforgettable; also the time Rinus Michels, now
national coach to the Dutch team, spent with the club,
and Hannes Löhr.

Michels was a real tough guy, both deeply hated and
respected – by at least 90 percent of the players. He was
even more strict than Weisweiler. Training with him was
genuine torture: there was exercise drill, running until you
dropped, all 'gingered up' with a variety of insults.

My friends Pierre Littbarski and Klaus Allofs found it
deeply offensive. They seethed with anger and felt they
were being treated like slaves. There was revolution in the

air. The atmosphere was rife with frustration and discontent. The changing rooms rang with remarks such as 'It's typical Dutch arrogance towards us Germans,' or 'He's a swine, a brutal swine.'

Just as Beckenbauer made some ill-advised remarks about the national team in Mexico in 1986 because he was feeling frustrated, Michels also let off steam about the poor quality of his players: he was scornful, humiliated them, and gave them all a dressing-down. Before long I was the only member of the Cologne team who had a good word to say for him.

Since it was just me against everybody else, I couldn't stop the rebellion. One day Michels complained to the board about the poor quality of players; he wanted to buy some good mature players if the team was to achieve any success again. At the same time, he blocked all the board's initiatives to introduce a new strategy: they wanted to buy young, as yet immature, talent that would develop into star quality at Cologne. I personally favoured the board's proposals. As a result, I have to admit I left Michels in the lurch. Michels couldn't survive after that. Sadly, I had a hand in his departure, although his diagnosis of the club seemed very accurate to me: as far as laziness and dilettantism were concerned, he was absolutely right. I regretted his leaving. Michels was one of the few people in the club whom I spent time with socially; we would have dinner together with our wives, or go to the opera.

I saw him again in August 1986, in Eindhoven, in Holland, at the award ceremony for the Footballer of the Year Award. He was still very friendly towards me, which pleased me greatly. Like so many coaches who take their jobs seriously, he'd had a serious heart attack.

Apart from Weisweiler and Michels, I also rank Branko Zebec and Ernst Happel – the former and present coaches of HSV – among the profession's elite. All four set the players absolute standards, and treat their stars with brutal contempt. Branko Zebec, for instance, picked up a handful of stones after a bad match to determine how many times the players had to run round the pitch for punishment. Each stone represented one circuit, and they had to do it. No one dared grumble, and not one of the world-class players opened his mouth to complain.

Do the worst sadists make the best coaches? The two inevitably go together, though the public may not like it. It shouldn't have to be that way. If coaches didn't have to combat laziness and dilettantism they could afford to be more humane *and* get good performances from their players.

A fair comparison between players would stimulate their ambition and spur them on to greater heights. As things stand, everyone thinks he's the best – when in fact he's mediocre, if not in terms of form, then technically. Too many players are bone idle – and too many coaches as well! Large numbers of 'professionals' bank anything between 10,000 and 30,000 marks a month despite the most lamentable performances. We're dealing with a 'conspiracy of laziness' between players and coaches. And once again, this reinforces the board of directors' power over the coaches, who lay themselves open to criticism. The Bundeslige is a real powder-keg. And it's no wonder that in these inauspicious circumstances the whole thing might blow up at the least 'short-circuit' in the system.

The fact of the matter is that in clubs with an annual turnover of between five million and twenty million marks the players often don't know what they'll be doing the following week. There's no schedule, no training programme to give them some kind of overview. No holidays are fixed in advance. This was the state of affairs at HSV before Magath's time, and in Cologne until Kessler's arrival in 1985. Clearly, a great number of professional football players are unable to organize their lives on any rational basis because too many clubs are run by dilettantes.

No circus could afford to have the kind of amateurish management that is running most of the Bundeslige clubs. It would lead to chaos in the ring: lions and hippopotamuses would be biting each other, the monkeys would be annoying the elephants, the tigers would polish off the parrots! The big top would never be raised and taken down within a single day. Instead of one hundred performances a year, there would only be twenty, if that.

Hard to believe but true: dilettantism wherever you look. Only a few clubs – Bayern Munich for one – function smoothly. You can judge a management's quality by what happens when a player is injured. The contrast between different clubs is enormous:

– Thomas Kroth of HSV spent fourteen days in hospital, in Cologne, after his operation. During all that time, he received no visitors from his club, no telephone call, no letter, no flowers, no books – nothing. Neither from Dr Klein, President of the club, and still less from Günter Netzer. His prospective manager, Felix Magath, was the only one who called him up – from Mexico, 12,000 kilometres away!

– in Munich, the Bayern player Raimund Aumann suffered a torn cartilage. He was immediately taken to a Swiss university clinic. His manager, Uli Hoeness, took care of everything: the flight, the taxi, accommodation for Mrs Aumann in Zürich.

The way you're taken care of when you're ill is absolutely crucial in professional football. The players may earn a lot of money, but their injuries and afflictions are shrugged off by other people as 'occupational hazards'.

This can't go on.

Herbert Neumann, Rüdiger Schmitz and I have founded a sports agency. I see this as a chance for the future. We're already advising and looking after top sportsmen. In time, we want to organize sports competitions and launch various projects. Our agency will become a kind of laboratory where proposals for reform in sport can be tried out and tested. Working outside, indeed in opposition to, the DFB bureaucracy.

We would like to build a rehabilitation centre for injured players. How many times have I seen sick players treated by coaches and managers as though they were good for the scrap-heap. They're just abandoned. We would need a team of people including a doctor – possibly Professor Schneider, the chief consultant at a clinic for sports injuries in Cologne who has already operated on me twice, or Professor Steinhäuser, chief consultant at a hospital in Zülpich; and also a qualified sports instructor able to provide physiotherapy and special exercises; in addition to our masseur Dieter Siegmund and Heinz Flohe to teach football technique. Then we would be able to encourage and develop young talent as well. Our sports agency and talent scouts would become a nursery for future players in the national team.

12

SPORT:
A MULTIMILLION-DOLLAR
BUSINESS

DWINDLING GATES, clubs in dire financial straits, well into
the red, their assests invested in property and melting
away like snow in the sunshine. Apart from a few fortunate
exceptions, nearly all the clubs are affected by the crisis.
Among the lucky ones are Bayern Munich (a very well-
managed club) and Leverkusen (which has the backing of
the Firma company). But advertising revenue and income
from selling television broadcasting rights are not enough
to overcome the clubs' financial problems.

Money, so it's said, is the central nerve of war. As far as
football is concerned, money is not the most important
nerve, but it is an integral part of the nervous system. The
desire to dispel the spectre of bankruptcy has inspired our
hopeful young managers with very bold ideas. Manfred
Ommer, a tax consultant by profession who happens to be
President of FC Hamburg, has been particularly cunning.
'Why don't we register our footballers as capital investments?' this smart man very shrewdly asked. Fascinating
idea. People as mobile investment? Capital on legs? How

flattering to the Bundeslige players. This startlingly original idea has been practised by Texan financiers since pioneering days: they invested in four-legged mobile capital – large herds of cattle, as every well-informed fan of the Western knows. Footballers to be written off as tax losses? No.

Professional football is in the grip of some very ruthless business interests. The sport itself has been relegated to the background while business interests prevail. Advertising brings money into the clubs and the money enables the clubs to perform well and be successful. Their success confirms their attraction to sponsors, boosting their appeal. The value of the kicking, two-legged advertisement-carriers soars. This is roughly how the business side of the football world operates. Sport is so closely bound up with advertising paid for by industry that neither can survive any more without the other. 'Professional sport and industry have the same relationship with one another as a hanged man with the rope,' say the cynics.

'Industry' is a very vague term in this context. Let's call a spade a spade: Adidas and Puma. These two companies are like super-powers in the world market for sportswear; they confront each other like the Americans and the Soviets during the Cold War.

Adidas and Puma between them control the lion's share (80 percent) of this world market; Adidas with an annual turnover of 4 billion marks, Puma with 1.5 billion, and increasing for both market leaders. Outside these giants' sphere of influence, there's practically nothing. It must be made quite clear: no sports club of any kind, whether in Western Europe, Africa or Asia, can develop without one of these two companies getting in on the act.

They know what huge sums of money can be earned

through sport – which is why Puma and Adidas will fight tooth and nail for a share of the spoils.

Health and beauty through sport – it certainly sounds good.

'People are body-conscious,' I read in the newspapers and magazines. Body-building studios are springing up like mushrooms. Sport is 'in', no one can be unaware of it. In 1974 only 4 percent of my fellow citizens took part in any sport; today the figure is nearly 18 percent.

Nearly one fifth of people's income is spent on their leisure-time activities. For companies that produce sports equipment of any kind a golden age has dawned: the market is growing at an annual rate of 8 percent. In the early 80s the market seemed saturated; but since 1985 the industry has been expanding rapidly. The number of 20- to 30-year-olds will continue to increase until 1990. And it seems to be a generation that isn't particularly inclined to bring children into the world, but is more interested in cultivating their own bodies. These up-coming generations will be extremely active and leisure-conscious. And so the sports industries reckon on doubling their annual turnover, which already stands at 145 billion marks, by the year 2000.

It doesn't take a great deal of imagination to picture the kind of feverish avarice a market forecast like this will stimulate. Every club president is faced with a very simple choice: Adidas or Puma? That's how powerful they are today. The idea of a free choice is just a joke: the president can only choose which of the two he is going to become dependent on. I call that a free choice of prison. The DFB has opted for Adidas, so the national eleven wear the famous three stripes and the Adidas flower logo. All the big names in German football are wedded to Adidas: and foremost among them is Franz Beckenbauer, the perfect

public relations manager for the company. Football fans
know that Breitner, Rummeniggee and myself all wear the
Adidas logo. Malicious tongues talk of Adidas's national
team. In a cover story in *Der Spiegel* we were lampooned as
a national eleven whose paymasters were Adidas – we
were depicted all sitting in an Adidas shoebox. Uli Stein
once again missed the chance to keep one of his inane
remarks to himself. After he'd been kicked out of the
World Cup team, he said (with that familiar expression on
his pointed face – that of the fox in the fable who couldn't
reach the grapes hanging above its head): 'Beckenbauer,
Neuberger and Adidas – now there's a team that works
well together. The only thing they're interested in is keeping Schumacher, another Adidas man, in goal.'

Remarks like this reveal the quality of what Little Uli
has between his ears.

All the national players are obliged to wear Adidas kit
the moment they start playing for Germany.

Those players who have individual promotion contracts with Puma – such as Völler, Matthäus or Allofs –
have to leave their Puma shirts in the changing rooms
when they go into an international stadium with the
national side.

For the Adidas managers, who, God knows, are no
choirboys, it's a source of fiendish delight to be able to
hijack the Puma players like this. It's doubly gratifying
when 1.5 billion viewers watch them on television wearing
the distinctive Adidas emblem, as they did during the last
World Cup in Mexico.

In the past decade Adidas has managed to get the best
and most popular footballers to join the Adidas team.
Nothing, not a single thing, has been left to chance. There
is not even the remotest possibility of Puma's being able to
challenge them as long as Beckenbauer, Breitner and

Overath have any say in the matter. That's the way it is.

In return Adidas equip both the football stars and the young newcomers to the clubs. An expensive privilege.

Other firms are free to try the same, and they might offer in addition an annual fee to the sportsmen and clubs. Puma spares no effort in trying to recruit players and clubs signed up by Adidas with the offer of huge sums of money. The explanation for the very high income and fantastic salaries enjoyed by some of the stars undoubtedly lies in these offers. Maradona earns about one million Deutschmarks a year from Puma, and his contract runs for five years. Rudi Völler also has a five-year contract that will earn him nearly a quarter of a million marks every year – again with Puma.

In order not to lose us, Adidas has to keep pace, offering similarly large sums to Rummenigge, Beckenbauer and myself. So far, so good. That's how competition works.

. Adidas and other firms have recouped their investment in German football one hundred times over. For the past ten years, after all, we've been at the top of the world league. Basically, no price can be put upon the publicity gained through the national side. And the managers at Herogenaurach, the town where Adidas has its head office, know it. For years they've been enjoying an 8 percent growth rate, opening up new markets as they are now doing in Asia, for instance. And this success does not come by accident. Puma too are fully aware that clubs like Werder Bremen, Borussia Mönchengladbach and Fortuna Düsseldorf have contributed to the company's success, represented by an annual turnover of 1.5 billion marks, and an annual increase in sales of about 10 percent.

I've been very struck by the effect that Boris Becker has had on the tennis industry. Puma, who supply our young star with the rackets he plays with, now sell ten times as many rackets as before. After Becker won the Wimbledon title they couldn't keep up with demand. The volume of tennis equipment sold totals around 300 million marks – thanks to Becker. If he had only a 10 percent share of this tennis boom, he would have been earning 30 million marks a year. It's completely crazy, of course. Figures of this kind defy comprehension, and it all becomes rather unreal.

But plenty of professional sportsmen are not invited to take part in this orgy of money. It leads to envy, jealousy, enmity. And something ought to be done about it. I'm in favour of an equitable sharing of the spoils. In other words, all the money should be put into a kitty and divided into twenty-two equal lots. That way, even the players who have to sit out the game on the bench will get their share. This would be a fair solution worth introducing for the sake of peace. I would subscribe to it. Personal contracts would not be affected, since they depend on the individual's personal talent, dedication and market value. I'm delighted whenever another player lands a contract. And the reason's obvious: the more publicity there is surrounding us, the more we'll all earn. It's a snowball effect, and not a cause for professional jealousy. However, not many people share my view. The envious sportsman feels cheated as soon as a fellow player starts earning money a bit faster than he is. But it's inevitable that only those who are outstanding performers are going to be courted by sponsors.

Sport, publicity, the national coach: the relationship of power between these three explains Franz Beckenbauer's return to the world of football. A very courageous decision on his part. We really weren't much of a team then. We wanted to become world champions, or runners-up to the champions, but the dream had so far eluded us. Franz only stood to lose, but he went ahead and made that brave transition from player to coach. He did this for us, and of course for his own financial advantage. That also is quite legitimate.

On the plane returning from a game abroad, Franz came and sat next to me.

'I'm quitting. After the '86 World Cup,' he said emphatically. 'Definitely. It's too stressful, too much trouble. I'd rather play tennis or golf.'

I was unsympathetic. 'That's just great. You take on the job of running the team and get all the publicity contracts under your belt. And once the money's in your pocket you say: "Goodbye, gentlemen. It's been nice working with you." '

Franz stared at me, somewhat annoyed. 'Are you crazy? I had contracts long before I took the job. Plenty of them.'

'Don't talk rubbish,' I replied. 'You may have had three contracts, but not seven or eight as you do now. And you got them because of your job.'

Beckenbauer burst out laughing, wondering which of us was 'the predator'. We understood each other.

I think he's perfectly entitled to the money he gets. I would like all my colleagues to earn a lot. After all, I know that by the age of thirty-five most of us are finished, without any real profession, and physically pretty wrecked. Footballers retire early and have to earn as much as they can while they're active.

You aren't born with a sponsorship contract. I started in a small way. I wasn't yet very well known when the glove manufacturers Reusch, based in the Black Forest, offered me 2,000 Deutschmarks a year for the pleasure of wearing their gloves. A very nice extra bit of income.

Only after we won the European Championship in Rome in 1980 did the offers become really exciting. Already during the championship Rüdiger Schmitz was negotiating with Adidas on my behalf. If I put up a good show and our team won the title then there was the prospect of a contract. That was my breakthrough. I knew that only players in the national side could hope for a contract and benefit from deals worth 100,000 marks and more a year. I later signed a contract with Adidas, whereby the more they sold, the more I earned. When I got my first cheque from Adidas I was very pleasantly surprised.

My name was not much good for promoting shoes, but shirts are altogether another matter – I even help design them. I regularly visit the Adidas head offices and work with the company on the latest collections. I try to advise as a 'consumer'. I might make suggestions along the lines of: 'Why don't you make the stripes diagonal?' The size, the cut, the roominess, where the padding needs to go, the choice of fabric – I thoroughly enjoy being involved in deciding all of these things. And my contribution helps the industry cater better to the wishes and requirements of sportsmen.

The glove manufacturers Reusch take even more notice of my suggestions. I have watched the gloves being made, and I'm astonished by the skill of the workers. The gloves are always being improved. Gebhard Reusch takes my most radical ideas seriously.

My real coup came to me on a double-decker bus in London one day: there I was sitting in front of a glass plaque that was stuck to a sheet of rubber. There were no suckers or frame holding the glass in position, but it didn't slip or slide. It was bomb-proof. Very impressed by this, I tore off a little piece of this rubber (I know, I'm a vandal!)

and took it back to Mr Reusch. He had his chemists analyze it. The amazing upshot of this was that since then, that substance, which is incredibly absorbant in damp weather, has been used in the manufacture of gloves that bear my name.

Industrial espionage? Not really. Just a goalkeeper's reflex action.

After Adidas, other sponsors came knocking at my door. A pharmaceutical company had developed a product that worked miracles. Applied to bumps, bruises and swellings, it brought immediate relief. Even the Americans contacted me to do some publicity: McDonalds had me biting into a hamburger on hoardings that were several metres high.

After the '82 World Cup and my 'foul' against Battiston my popularity declined for a while. Having fallen from favour, I was regarded as a swine. Who's going to sign up a thug for publicity? One thing that helped save me from bankruptcy was a letter from Alf Bente, one of the Adidas executives, who dealt with the national team.

Bente wrote to me, saying more or less the following: we would like to continue working together. Everyone makes mistakes. The thing is to put them behind you as quickly as possible. I'm sure that you will. We still have confidence in you.

Alf did not try to gloss over things. He stuck with me despite the scandal. You don't betray partners like that. That's why, when the Adidas–Puma power-struggle broke out inside FC Cologne's senior team, I stood by them.

13

THE ADIDAS–PUMA WRANGLE

IT SELDOM pays to be overconfident. The trouble began in 1984: Adidas took it for granted that FC Cologne's senior team would carry their logo forever. Why shouldn't it, after all, with Wolfgang Overath very successfully representing the company in the North Rhineland–Westfalen region? Adidas became careless about the amount of sympathy it could count on within the club, while the Puma people unobtrusively began their PR campaign, cultivating their contacts at all levels – with players, trainers and directors. The board of FC Cologne was invited to visit the Puma works – on a completely open-ended basis, of course, with no commitment on either side. Nobody seriously thought that the club would change its allegiance to Puma. Negotiations between Adidas and Cologne were already scheduled. Werner von Moltke, head of PR at Adidas, and Wolfgang Overath had already prepared the ground, having both conducted lengthy discussions with Peter Weiand, President of the club, and everything was agreed in principle. It only remained for the Cologne officials concerned to go to Herzogenaurach to sign the contract.

Horst Dassler, Adidas's chief executive, was represented at the meeting by Dr Martens. The new contract was lying on the table.

'Unfortunately, Martens knew nothing about football, nor did he have the right psychological approach. He was too pedantic,' the Cologne people complained afterwards. Through a number of little ruses and so-called negotiating techniques, Martens tried to introduce changes to the new contract and even to delete some clauses. The Cologne representatives felt they were being conned and they didn't like it.

Adidas later maintained that they had acted in good faith all along. There were simply a few details that needed clarifying and this was the object of the meeting in Herzogenaurach. One thing is certain: the talks went on for hours before a settlement was reached. The contract had yet to be signed, but it was late and the whole document had to be retyped.

'Never mind,' said the Cologne people (according to Adidas), 'we're not in any hurry. We can sign the contract tomorrow.'

They all shook hands on it.

All part of some strategy? Or a misunderstanding? In any case, there was mistrust on both sides.

At that time Cologne also had an offer on the table from Puma. It was worth millions, as was the Adidas offer. The club's board of directors considered it only courteous to inform Armin Dassler, Puma's chief executive, that same evening, of the deal that had apparently been struck with Adidas.

Puma is also based at Herzogenaurach. The head of Puma is called Armin Dassler; the Dassler who runs

Ad¡das is his cousin Horst. The two men can't stand each other.

The Cologne people paid a flying visit to Puma, and were very warmly received. The company director was courteous, friendly and obliging. A real gentleman. Knowing Peter Weiand and how susceptible he is to being soft-soaped, I'm sure he must have relished it. After the cold-shower treatment at Adidas, where only an 'apprentice sorcerer' – and a pendantic, impudent nitpicker at that – had time to see the Cologne delegation, at Puma they were received by the smiling boss himself, who took the news of having lost out to Adidas in exemplarily dignified fashion.

Later, on the way home, the Cologne people grew sentimental and started having second thoughts. They voiced doubts as to whether the lordly Adidas boss was really the right partner for them.

During the following week Peter Weiand got the FC Cologne board to cancel their agreement with Adidas. Fresh negotiations with Puma got under way, with Armin Dassler standing by his attractive offer. Adidas threatened to take legal action; Weiand got upset and dug his heels in. Puma eventually carried the day – and all because Adidas had forgotten the most basic rules of business psychology. It was as simple as that.

Life became hellishly difficult for me as an Adidas supporter through a debt of gratitude. As my contract with Cologne states very clearly, everything I do while I'm with the club is subject to their approval – whether it's a matter of signing autographs or an endorsement contract. The club had signed up with Puma. It was inconceivable that any player should not toe the line.

'According to the terms of our contract, all the players, without exception, must wear the Puma logo!' insisted

Armin Dassler, quite understandably. 'I cannot allow any one to be exempted.'

I was caught in an impossible situation. Remaining loyal to Adidas meant kicking Puma in the shins. There followed ten meetings with Cologne's board of directors, and endless sessions with Michael Meier, the Manager of Cologne's senior team. My contract with Adidas ran until 31 December 1986. The agreement between Puma and the club came into effect from July 1985. What was I to do? I certainly couldn't go and play stark naked in goal just to avoid giving offence to either party.

The wrangle became increasingly insoluble, soon resembling a kind of trench warfare. Sticking by Adidas meant having to leave my club. But I also had the option of extending my contract with Cologne for a further three years. In which case I would have to abandon Adidas. I could see no satisfactory way out of this dilemma, and the media again had a field day with stories about 'Schumacher the troublemaker'.

One evening a call came through on Rüdiger Schmitz's phone. It was Armin Dassler on the line.

'This to-ing and fro-ing has been going on far too long,' said the Puma chief. 'I suggest we talk it over once more, somewhere quiet. I'd like to make you another offer regarding Toni Schumacher.'

'I'm very sorry, Mr Dassler,' replied Rüdiger. 'It's very kind of you, but any discussions between us would be pointless. We won't abandon Adidas – we'd sooner leave Cologne.'

Nevertheless, on Dassler's insistence, a meeting was fixed for the following day at the Hotel Excelsior in Cologne.

Quite obviously, Puma's chief executive was preparing another charm-offensive, of the kind he'd launched on our board of directors some time before, at Herzogenaurach. He received us in a hotel suite, and was both obliging and understanding.

'I appreciate what a difficult position you're in, Mr Schumacher. A real dilemma. It's not my intention to back you into a corner. I want to offer you a truly attractive alternative. What I propose is . . .'

At this point I interrupted Mr Dassler and asked him if he would be kind enough to deal with Rüdiger Schmitz on this issue. At that time I found any business discussions of this nature extremely awkward and embarrassing. They made me feel as though I was having to step outside of myself. Despite all Rüdiger's efforts, I had so far successfully avoided getting involved in any negotiations with Cologne. Just the thought of having to 'sell' myself – to show off and claim to be the best, the most marvellous – makes my hair stand on end and my skin crawl. Perhaps if I played Tarzan and swung from the chandelier, it would impress people!

It's a ghastly business. Embarrassing. Absurd. I've never been able to bring myself to do it. The person I'd have to deal with would naturally try to get me as cheaply as possible and make out that I was small and unimportant, belittling my talents. I can see only two possibilities at that point: either I attack the guy, or else I slink off with my tail between my legs. It's much easier for Rüdiger to handle negotiations. Not being the person concerned, he doesn't get annoyed.

I can still hear myself saying: 'I'll sit and listen, Mr Dassler, but Rüdiger Schmitz will speak for me.'

'As you wish,' said Dassler, all smiles, turning to Rüdiger. 'It just isn't on for one Cologne player not to wear our logo. I cannot allow any exceptions. Especially when the player concerned is the best goalkeeper in Germany.'

'It's very flattering of you to say so,' replied my manager, 'but we intend to remain loyal to Adidas. That's the way we are. I see no solution to the problem, and as I said to you on the phone yesterday, I'm afraid this discussion won't get us any further forward – although we're delighted to meet you here in Cologne.'

Armin Dassler laughed and continued to be friendly and obliging.

'Wait,' he said. 'You don't know yet what my offer is.'

'If it's money that you're thinking of offering, it won't change our minds.'

'Money is just an indication of a star player's worth. Toni is a very big star. I want him. For Puma. For myself. As a matter of honour. Money in itself doesn't mean anything to me.'

We didn't say anything.

'As evidence of my esteem for Toni, I'm prepared to offer much more than Adidas: I'm offering the sum of . . .'

Rüdiger and I couldn't believe our ears. We had never even dreamed of such a fantastic offer. Dassler was talking about a huge sum of money, and he was tactfully presenting it as a token of friendship. Even Rüdiger looked a bit stunned. He was embarrassed, not wanting to offend Dassler. But he had to.

'Impossible,' he said. 'Absolutely impossible. Our credibility is at stake.'

Dassler's face betrayed enormous disappointment, but he displayed admirable self-control. We all sat there feeling horribly uncomfortable and awkward.

Armin Dassler saw us down to the hotel entrance and wished us all the best when we parted.

After walking a few paces, I groaned: 'Rudiger, that's the last time I take part in any negotiations.'

'Why's that?'

'It's pointless, I knew all along that I was going to stick with Adidas.'

'So what? You also have to learn what other people think of loyalty.'

'Thank God we stood our ground. Changing allegiance wasn't something I'd ever seriously considered.'

'Right. But it just goes to show what good lads we are,' Rüdiger said happily.

I felt completely drained. Worse than after three day's training. But we still hadn't come up with a solution to my problem. There seemed only one possible course of action: to get a transfer. But where to?

I was prepared to move to France, Spain, or Italy. We'd already been in contact with Paris St Germain. I simply had to bide my time, concentrate on my game and on training, and switch to an Adidas-sponsored club.

Who would give way? Would Cologne renege on its contract with Puma? That was inconceivable. Perhaps Puma would waive the contract? Hardly. Maybe Adidas would sell me to Puma? Stranger things have happened. But I would have found this alternative humiliating. However, anything was possible.

Eventually the club made me another offer, a fair one: they would extend my contract for a further four years, from June 1985, on condition that Puma, FC Cologne and Adidas reached some agreement over my case.

'Naturally we'll give you time to think it over,' Michael Meier, the club manager, told me.

The Cologne carnival was then in full swing. Perhaps I should have put on a clown's mask and wandered incognito through the streets to escape my worries. . .

A few days later I was at Herzogenaurach, going over Adidas's new collection. On the way back, Rüdiger's car-phone rang. It was Marlies, sounding very anxious.

'I think something's up, but I don't know what it is. Journalists keep ringing up to congratulate you on your new contract with Cologne. I'm beginning to find it rather sinister. Why all these phone calls? Is it some kind of test? Are they trying to steam-roller you into wearing Puma's colours for the club?'

I was completely nonplussed. Rüdiger too. Were they trying to present us with a *fait accompli*? Was the carnival party that evening of 11 February 1985 some kind of trap? Should I not go?

'You must go,' Rüdiger decided. 'Shirking the issue is no solution. In any case, a carnival party is no place to sign a contract.'

I put on my dinner jacket as though it were a coat of mail and made my way to the Sartory reception rooms, where the party was to take place. Michael Meier was there waiting for me.

He said solemnly: 'Harald, we've done it. We've been having talks with Dassler all afternoon. Weiand and I have got Puma to agree to let you go. You can stay with Adidas.'

How can a company 'let you go' when you've never worked for them? Alarmed, I decided to ring Rüdiger at once. I found a telephone in the hotel kitchens where I could make my call undisturbed.

'I'm not having anything to do with this pantomime that Weiand and Dassler are trying to stage. They're not going to get me dancing to their tune. Not even during carnival.'

I could hear my team-mates being applauded. They were now Puma employees.

'Don't play their game,' said Rüdiger. 'Step outside. It'll do you good to get some fresh air and smoke a cigarette. Let them get on with it, but whatever you do, don't get riled.'

I had a flock of journalists on my heels but I managed to give them the slip.

There were embarrassed faces at the party.

'It's Toni getting his revenge on my husband for not letting him play in the match against Waldorf Mannheim,' said Mrs Weiand. 'Peter interrupted the run of matches Toni had appeared in and deprived him of the chance to break the record.'

It's true that I was angry with Cologne's President on that issue; I still am.

In the autumn of 1984 I gave an interview to a press agency in which I criticised Cologne's policy of buying in players. The board wanted to teach me a lesson.

'Schumacher is out of the match against Mannheim,' was the harsh sentence meted out to me. Dr Worms, a member of the management committee, Mr Schäfer, the club's legal adviser, Rüdiger Schmitz and I all tried to persuade Peter Weiand to waive the suspension.

Eventually my supporters got the impression that the President was coming round. At three o'clock in the morning, it seemed he had.

'Weiand is expecting you at his house at eight o'clock sharp. With all your kit,' Mr Schäfer told me.

Was the whole thing settled? A few hours later, on the stroke of eight, I was on the President's doorstep. He looked at me peevishly, was obviously a bit embarrassed, and then delivered the bombshell: 'Toni, I'm sorry but you can't go to Mannheim – your suspension hasn't been lifted.'

I thought I hadn't heard him correctly. He couldn't possibly mean it. But Weiand just stood there, looking uncomfortable.

Like a helpless father with a rebellious son, he just didn't want to lose face. That's the only possible explanation I could find to account for his sudden change of mind; at three o'clock in the morming he'd thought differently.

Peter Weiand is actually old enough to be my father. I think of him as a person worthy of every respect, and in fact I'm really rather fond of him. He's just as impulsive and difficult to restrain as I am; he's very volatile and as vain as a peacock – he can't bear being criticised. We've often crossed swords; I can't stand the way he stands on his dignity and he can't take my insolence.

But to get back to the suspension: I had set my mind on playing four hundred consecutive matches, without missing a single one, and breaking my hero Sepp Maier's record.

Despite injury, I had already played a continuous series of 213 games, achieved in six successive years of professional football, playing 34 matches a year. And then my own club president smashed my dream to bits.

However, the suspension had nothing to do with that carnival evening in Cologne.

Michael Meier telephoned Rüdiger while I smoked the cigarette I'd been prescribed. Wolfgang Overath, who was Carnival Prince that year, formally requested me to make an appearance on the platform. No one can deny a prince his wish. So I agreed. President Weiand was very tactful and made no reference to the contract. First thing next day, the deal with Puma was officially announced. Armin Dassler continued to behave chivalrously, and never mentioned anything about the concessions he'd made or about 'letting me go', at least not in my presence. Everyone's honour was saved.

More and more European clubs are being adopted by international concerns that want to improve their own image. In France, for instance, the Paris Racing Club has signed a contract with Jacques Lagarder, the president of

Matra, one of the giants in the electronics and arms industries. Similarly, Marseilles Olympic has been signed up by the Frenchman Bernard Tapie, a live-wire industrialist. In Germany, Uerdingen and Leverkusen are 100 per cent financed by the pharmaceutical company Bayer, whilst Bayern Munich's function is to promote the image of Commodore Computers – whenever he appears on the German TV programme *Sport-Studio*, Bayern's coach Udo Lattek makes sure his interviews have a 'Commodore look'.

It's no longer a two-horse race, with just Adidas and Puma. Major companies in other areas of industry are also interested in wooing players. A star player can be commercialized from head to toe. The advertising on shirts that you used to get seems very modest compared with the way shirts are now completely plastered with the names of well-known products.

It is no coincidence that Pierre Littbarski was lured away to Paris Racing Club, that Marseilles were interested in Karl-Heinz Förster, or that Brehme joined Munich for 2 million DM, the highest transfer fee of the 1986–7 season. The Germans and the French are not the only ones taking part in these big transfer deals. The Spanish and Italian clubs are also very quick off the mark in the competition to buy star players. Barcelona, Madrid, Milan and Turin are always outbidding each other, offering astronomical sums to acquire new players. The German clubs are finding it increasingly difficult to hold their own. They see their best players going abroad and the Bundeslige becoming increasingly impoverished of star quality, and they are powerless to prevent it.

This is the so-called 'free market'. But why should we necessarily accept it? Our best engineers have already been enticed away to America; the same thing happened with our physicists some time ago, when there was a real exodus. Our scientists emigrate to countries where they can earn four times what they earn here.

In football, there is a paradoxical reversal of roles between the North and the South. It's the poorest countries that pay the highest transfer fees. In Italy, France and Spain, football is the most popular spectator sport of all. There's an element of 'opium of the people' about it. In Naples, apparently, there are football fans, some of them unemployed, who go without food in order to pay for their ticket into the football ground.

From the tax point of view, it's a much more attractive proposition to live in Italy during your football career. If top earners didn't have to pay tax at a rate of 56 per cent in Germany, I'm sure that far fewer of my colleagues would opt to go abroad.

I too was tempted to leave Germany – in 1985, when I was embroiled in the Puma–Adidas wrangle. As well as exploring the possibilities with Paris St Germain, I was also dreaming of the sun in Naples, of the 100,000 wildly enthusiastic fans in Barcelona, where I would also have been with my friend Bernd Schuster again. Nothing came of it. There isn't as much demand for goalkeepers as there is for strikers and forwards, unfortunately – perhaps mistakenly? I have often discussed the matter with Bernd Schuster.

'If you'd joined us at Barcelona,' he said, 'we would undoubtedly have been league champions three years running and Barcelona would certainly have won the European Cup. The Spanish and Italians have a much higher regard for the player who scores than for the man who saves a goal. If a player in either of these countries scores a hat-trick in a game, the newspapers the next day devote four whole pages to the story. A goalkeeper who saves three penalties will only get a couple of lines. It's ridiculous, but absolutely typical of the Spanish. Saving goals instead of scoring doesn't really mean much to the crowd, the players, or club managers.'

Schuster was right: Spain wouldn't have been the right place for me.

14

FOOTBALL AS A
SPECTATOR SPORT

IF ALL the world's a stage, then the stadium is the stage *par excellence*. And yet fewer and fewer people are prepared to go to this theatre. Dwindling gate figures are the latest problem facing football clubs. The reasons for the fall-off in attendance are common knowledge: not enough star players to draw spectators, competition from television, the high cost of a ticket to see a game, hooliganism, poor standards of play . . .

All of this is true, but only partly to blame. No one mentions the agony of sitting on rusty slatted benches, or of standing on open terraces, where everyone is bound to catch a cold. No one complains about being served luke-warm beer in paper cups, or about the unappetizing limp sandwiches at the price of caviar. Who ever mentions the hours you have to spend stuck in a traffic jam, the miles you have to trek from the car park to the stadium? It's quite unacceptable. OK, the games are often not up to much, but the facilities for spectators are just not good enough, and this situation should not be allowed to continue. Things must change.

In an interview with *Stern* magazine, Neuberger, the President of the DFB, made a number of good suggestions: the seating should be more comfortable – not just some rough old planks with nails sticking out of them; there should be better parking, nearer the stadium, and fewer expanses of concrete – the stadiums are too stark.

At a time when people have an increasing amount of leisure time at their disposal, and the leisure industry is expanding, the stadium of the future should be a place designed for the whole family. Ideally, there should be some kind of leisure park around the stadium, with lawns, playing fields, a shopping centre, a swimming pool, restaurants and cafés. And if I had my way, the stadiums would be quickly and easily accessible, and situated away from the traffic chaos in towns. You could begin by introducing better signposting from the motorway exits to the grounds.

This must be the way forward. It's a disgrace that 50,000 spectators are kept waiting before and after a match with no provision made for their entertainment, on the grounds that it would cost too much – which is just an excuse for idleness. I'm convinced that commercial advertising departments would be delighted to sponsor entertainments of various kinds. During half-time, you could have choirs, actors like Millowitsch, a band, a dance show, and before the start of a match, maybe a car show – Mercedes, Opel and BMW would surely agree to take part. And after the match is over, why not have Peter Maffey to sing to the crowd?

Football would remain the main feature, without question. But other kinds of performers should provide the entertainment before and after. And then for ninety minutes – a really good game of football! It would take a considerable amount of effort to organize this; certainly it would be beyond the capabilities of the dilettantes running our clubs at present. These proposals aren't going to be put into practice within the coming year – it's a question of attitude. But we could begin by introducing a bit of electronic equipment into the stadiums: for instance, a giant video screen next to the scoreboard, so that spectators could watch action replays of the most exciting parts of the match, in close-up or slow motion. That would be one way of responding to the challenge from television. Never again should a football match end up being the kind of bloodbath that there was at the Heysel stadium in Belgium, in 1985. I didn't see it on television, but I can't stand pictures of violence, or of car accidents, fires, natural disasters, or war, and I would have switched it off if I'd been watching. What could the TV executives have been thinking of in allowing the broadcast to continue – it was sheer voyeurism of the most sickening kind.

This tragedy resulted from a number of cardinal errors of organization. It was irresponsible to let such fanatical supporters as the English and Italians into the stadium without any kind of search for offensive weapons. Security controls must be introduced. The authorities must never again be so culpably naïve. As in large political demonstrations, there's a hard core of professional troublemakers who want to see blood run. It's got to the stage where ordinary spectators are not coming to the matches, a state of affairs that could be remedied. Every measure must be taken to prevent any similar outbreak of violence in the future.

1. The way from the car park to the stadium should be clearly indicated, with good signposting and clear announcements over the loudspeakers.

2. The entrance ticket again should carry good, clear directions telling the spectator how to get into the stadium, which gate or terrace to go to, etc.

3. Potential adversaries among fanatical supporters should be rigorously kept apart, with Cologne supporters, for instance, in the south stand and visiting supporters at the north end. It's simply a matter of organization.

4. There should be as much police presence as necessary, especially at games considered 'explosive', to act as a deterrent. If everything is well organized, then nothing unforeseen will happen.

5. Anyone armed and potentially violent or drunk should not be allowed into the ground.

It is high time that something was done. New ideas and initiatives are called for. You can't put a stop to violence by simply deploring its existence. The most important thing is to ensure public safety and attract people back to the stadiums. It is no solution to the problem just to increase advertizing and publicity, or to ban the televising of matches. More imaginative measures are required.

Why not make it cheaper for fans who travel a long way to see a game – to show some appreciation for the 100 kms they have had to come? This would not only be fair but act as an incentive. Let's take Cologne as an example: fans who live in the city itself would pay 500 DM for their season ticket; those who have to travel 20 kms would pay 400 DM. There would be different travel zones – A, B, C etc. – up to a distance of 150 kms, with prices ranging from 500 to 120 DM. You'd be offering fans something concrete

– a mere 'thank you' to our supporters for their loyalty is not enough.

I can't understand why no one has come up with the idea before now. Income from the sale of broadcasting rights could help to make the entrance ticket cheaper. After all, the various TV channels are soon going to be bidding against one another for the exclusive right to televize Bundeslige matches.

Football, television and the drop in attendance figures – three factors in a difficult equation. More and more people are sitting down in front of the small screen – on Saturdays, 15–17 million. Conversely, there are fewer and fewer people on the terraces. In a very revealing article, the journalist Ulfert Schröder stated that on Saturdays, on average, sixty times more people watch the sport from their sofas than in the stadium. Over a whole season, German football attracts a total gate figure of about 6 million – barely one third of the TV viewers on a single Saturday. And this trend will only increase. It shouldn't be forgotten that in 1976 there was an average of 25,000 spectators per game; the figure for 1985–6 is 17,000. If this continues . . .

I'm not worried about the Bundeslige or the clubs; what they lose on the gate, they can make up on the sale of broadcasting rights – as much as 40 million DM per season. But it's easy to imagine this displacement of spectators resulting in an absurd state of affairs, with completely empty stadiums turned into TV studios, and games being played exclusively for the benefit of the cameras. What a nightmare! But I'm not that pessimistic. I believe that sooner or later, people are going to get fed up watching football on the box and they will start coming back to the stadiums. Before long, I expect to see a new balance between the number of spectators at the ground and those watching the game at home. But only if drastic reforms are introduced.

Is football itself still an enjoyable spectator sport, or should even the rules of the game be changed, as Franz Beckenbauer once jokingly implied? Some of the German coaches have some exotic ideas – Rudi Gutendorf, for instance, would like to see the goal posts set further apart. Others would like to abolish the offside rule. Everywhere people are talking of abolishing certain things and introducing others.

It's fairly obvious that one reason for the drop in attendance figures is the competition from television. But haven't the clubs also lost touch with their public? Have they not simply failed to realize that they must adapt to changed circumstances?

The harshness of the German winter doesn't really help. Having to take a break in midseason because of the weather costs the Bundeslige a great of money. Players, coaches, stadiums – everything is laid up but still has to be paid for. The bigger clubs, such as Hamburg, Munich or Cologne, are somewhat better off. We travel to Asia, Africa or, best of all, Latin America to play friendly matches. But there's talk of a simple solution to the problem: indoor football.

However, there are countless objections to it. The risk of injury is much greater playing on hard wood or even on a carpeted surface, however soft the carpet. We would rather play on frozen or snow-covered ground. And I'm not keen on swopping a pitch 120 metres long for a hall only 40 metres long. We might as well be given hockey sticks and have done with it!

Indoor football has so far only been played in friendly matches, so the games have tended to be restrained. But in a real contest the players would go all out to win. And then talk about the risk of injury! Not to mention the hysterical crowd, the shouting, the fireworks, the danger of fire – it doesn't bear thinking about.

I personally do not believe that indoor football in winter is the answer to the Bundeslige's problems. Along with my manager, Rüdiger Schmitz, I have something completely different in mind.

Our idea is to organize a Winter Championship. The prize would be a 'League Cup' that carries a large amount of money. We would need to build about four new stadiums in Germany, distributed around the country. These would belong to a new generation of designer stadiums with all the most up-to-date technical innovations. They would have a grass pitch, which would be the same size as a regular pitch; they would have perfect lighting, a removable roof-covering (that could be opened or closed depending on the weather), underground heating, and all the spectators would be seated. I can imagine such stadiums being built in Hanover, Nuremberg, Frankfurt and Cologne. The family would come to them, and children could be left in a crêche or play area, where they would be looked after. There would be shopping centres, hairdressing salons and dress shops for the ladies to go to while the men were cheering on the terraces . . .

Regardless of the weather, perhaps three games a week could be played in each of the four stadiums. With this Winter League Cup, football would recover its importance and re-establish itself as the major leisure activity in Germany. 'Holiday on Ice' was a great success – why shouldn't football do just as well?

The entrance fee would be kept down to somewhere between 5 and 20 DM. How would this be done? Quite simple: through sponsorship, advertizing and the sale of broadcasting rights. There would be no problems in financing a project of this kind. We've been negotiating for months with a Japanese company, working out detailed plans. We intend to instal giant video screens in the stadiums so that the most spectacular and best parts of any game can be replayed during half-time. In slow motion, of course.

15

THE PRESS

FOOTBALL WITHOUT the public is inconceivable – but just as inconceivable is football without the press. Popularity is the all-important issue. Every player is obsessed with the media. The same is also true of the DFB officials, who decided that relations with the press should be unprecedentedly harmonious during the 1986 World Cup in Mexico.

But putting both journalists and players under the same roof, at the Galinda Mansion, was a totally crazy idea, a grossly stupid arrangement that no one will ever dare attempt again. Even the journalists who originally wanted to be in the same hotel as the players eventually realized that it just couldn't work.

There were 140 journalists to 22 players and a few coaches and DFB officials, all in the same hotel in the middle of the country, cut off from the rest of the world. And while all we players wanted was a quiet life, the journalists, quite understandably, for professional reasons, were after some action, some lead stories and sensational exclusives.

And when there was absolutely nothing to report, these people became amazingly inventive. Even now, I can only marvel at what they came up with. I've got nothing against journalists. After all, they have to earn their living, with 70 lines about Beckenbauer here, 50 lines on Schumacher there . . .

Anyway, there were journalists lurking everywhere, lying in wait, scratching round for something to write about, racking their brains so as not to keep repeating the same nonsense. These poor guys already had each other to contend with, but on top of that their editors started putting pressure on them: 'I want a story and I want it now!'

The demand for news is insatiable; it thrives on rumour, crises and rows; it relishes scandals and gossip. But this is no reason why the national football team should act as saps to provide material for newspaper headlines. But this is precisely what the hungry horde of hacks reporting the World Cup wanted. And their wish was granted – in no small measure, unfortunately.

Rainer Holzschuh, the DFB press attaché, is a very nice young man. But he was completely unable to cope single-handed with 140 journalists. It's more than anyone could handle. He arranged and organized interviews between journalists, coaches and players, and held a daily press conference. No one could have been more friendly towards the press.

After lunch every day he would rush along the corridors, distributing assignments: 'Rummenigge – the *Süddeutche Zeitung*, Förster – *Der Bild*, Hoeness – DPA' (*Deutche Presse Agentur*, the German Press Agency), etc. I was also regularly involved. Before dinner we would talk to the press.

'Please be especially nice to Mr So-and-So from such-and-such a magazine; he's a really difficult customer.'

It could sometimes ruin your appetite. Especially when Franz Beckenbauer put his foot in it yet again.

The atmosphere was tense. As a diplomatic exercise, it was like having to walk across a highly polished parquet floor with bits of wet soap stuck to the soles of your shoes. Lots of journalists really tried hard to stir up trouble. By quoting startling and scandalous remarks that had allegedly been made, they tried to provoke spontaneous unguarded reactions from us. Just like a cat, I tried to slip away, to avoid the mob and dodge the traps.

Our encounters with the press took place in a typical Mexican inner courtyard, which was quickly dubbed the *Kontacthof* or 'contact yard' – the term used in German to describe the area where prostitutes meet their clients. We'd stand there like girls in a brothel – a little group here, some quiet whispering there – making secret assignations. I had only to speak to Rainer Kalb from *Kicker* magazine for two minutes and four of his 'dear colleagues' would be standing behind us, nostrils flaring at the scent of some mystery.

We were asked to be completely candid in our dealings with the press, so each of us was bound to find himself in an impossible situation on at least one occasion. The DFB hoped that this freedom of information would put them on a good footing with the press, assuming that the journalists were well disposed towards us. They could not have been more mistaken. The DFB achieved the exact opposite: a hint of jealousy was detected in the most harmless remark; a friendly slap on the back was interpreted as brawling. The journalists specialized in making mountains out of molehills. It was an absolute shambles. The reserve players were the only ones who benefitted. With so many journalists around, there was always one who would take an interest in them. And so they took advantage of the opportunity for a bit of PR – they certainly had plenty of time on their hands. Whereas the team that had actually been selected were busy – with the World Cup.

A national team without discord and strife is of no interest at all to the press. It was almost as though the editorial staff at head office were devising a few spicy dramas and that we then simply had to act out our assigned roles, playing either the aggrieved innocent or else the devil incarnate. The newspaper *Der Bild*, for instance, cast Karl-Heinz Rummenigge as the young male lead, playing the part of a Siegfried, with Beckenbauer as supporting male actor, and everyone else had just a bit-part. There was method in this coldly calculated attempt to manipulate public perceptions. The reader was to identify the World Cup in Mexico with Rummenigge. *Der Bild*'s reasoning was clear: what's important to the public? Who or what most attracts readers? The answers to these questions are decisive, and determine what the hacks working for the paper have to produce. On the whole, they're good people, Paul Breitner included, though there's a certain F.J. Wagner who writes feature articles for *Der Bild*: in-depth reports – exclusives, it goes without saying – consisting of amazing 'revelations'. After the World Cup I took the trouble to read a few of them. The stories are written in a very dramatic style that puts you in mind of Greek tragedy and is supposed to be terribly exciting. I found them dreadfully boring.

But that's enough criticism. There are some very good journalists – plenty of them.

Most of the reporters who work for agencies are good and also pretty civil. You can trust them to keep their word. The real professionals in the business include Bernd Linhoff of DPA, and Jürgen Leinemann and Kurt Röttgen from *Spiegel*. They are discreet, considerate, clever. I must also mention Ulfert Shröder, who is always the first to know everything. I respect and admire these men. They come and see you, listen to what you say and know how to keep quiet, when necessary.

Hans Eiberle of the *Süddeutchen Zeitung* writes very sound articles but his style is so dry and matter-of-fact that you feel as though you're reading an autopsy report. He's frightfully reserved, and he looked so morose walking the corridors of the Galinda Mansion that I never had the slightest desire to talk to him. In the seven weeks we were there, I didn't once see Eiberle smile.

Oskar Schmidt of the *Frankfurter Allgemeine Zeitung* is a more cheerful kind of guy, and very knowlegeable, but his reports are also a bit scholarly for my taste. He's a mine of information about football, but he can't help interpreting and analyzing. And then analyzing the analysis of the analysis . . . to the point where you can't understand a word.

There are many journalists, like Dettmar Cramer, known as 'Little Napoleon', who are capable of writing a 300-page book on 'The Free Kick' or 'The Corner'. I'm less impressed by this now than I used to be. Football is a simple game with simple rules: there are twenty players in the field, two goalkeepers, two goals, one ball, one referee. The object of the game is to kick the ball into your opponents' net. That's all there is to it. The offside rules are another story, admittedly. But why waste energy splitting hairs?

To return to Mexico: after dinner I would slip out the back way and go and find Rüdiger or return to my room. Not once did I go to the swimming pool, where the others usually spent their time. I didn't feel like it. I preferred not to hear about any intrigues, and if possible not to get involved in any through some ill-considered hasty remark, knowing how liable I am to shoot my mouth off. It was better that I stayed in my room reading or lifting weights.

We all know what fools actors can make of themselves when they take it into their head to write their own lines. So imagine the risk a footballer takes when he picks up a pen instead of sticking to the ball. But I'm no coward – and I won't let the fear of criticism put me off writing. In any case, the power of the press is a factor in sport that cannot be disregarded. Diversity of opinion, circulation figures – these are facts of life, and we footballers occasionally become the helpless prey these fickle newshounds set their sights on. And often they shit all over us, taking our performance, for what it's worth, as an excuse for displaying their talent – or lack of it – for rhetoric. We're the suckers. Always. The power and influence of the press are enormous – alarmingly so.

Hard to believe but true: if the press sets its mind to it, it can get a player a place in the national side; but it can just as easily get him kicked out of the team.

Before the 1980 World Cup in Rome, I benefitted from this. Whether I deserved it or not, I was virtually forced on Jupp Derwall by the press. In September 1986 I experienced the other side of the coin. Many journalists considered me 'finished'; and so I *was* 'finished'. 'Schumacher suffering crisis', 'Immel's Chance' . . . It was difficult not to be affected by things like this – the national coach found it even more difficult than me.

At the same time the hacks decided to make a star of Ludwig Kögl of Bayern Munich, by presenting him as the most popular and most talented player in the Bundeslige and getting him into the national team. There was a similar scenario before the World Cup, involving the defender Wolfgang Funkel of Uerdingen. Nobody gave a damn about Frank Neubarth of Bremen. Why not? Völler, Littbarski and Rummenigge were injured; that was the ideal opportunity to try out new players. With three of our forwards out of action, our team's front line was weak – but nobody suggested Frank Neubarth should go to Mexico. It was as though there was a kind of (unintentional?) campaign of disinformation going on; and there was no one lobbying for the Bremen player. On the other hand, we had some excellent players in defence, and yet all you read in the papers was how good Funkel was. He is good. But he's also got advocates prepared to lobby on his behalf – that's the minor detail that distinguishes him from Neubarth.

Another example: this time to show what a strain it can be living up to the high expectations built up by the press. Bernd Schuster, a very talented player, could not be persuaded to rejoin the national side. Because of his fear of the papers:

'. . . and what if I get off to a bad start? If I make a mistake?' he said, anxiously. 'Then the press who are praising me to the skies today will be damning me to hell tomorrow.'

He wasn't prepared to take the risk of taking a beating in Mexico. To me, this is an egotistical attitude. But I know who has a great influence over him: his wife Gabi wanted a quiet life for the family, no World Cup nonsense, no tensions. She wanted a holiday.

If newspapers like *Der Bild* or the Cologne *Express* keep publishing articles that begin with the question 'Why not player X or Y?' or 'Z deserves a chance and ought to be offered a place in the national side', then no coach can hold out against the headlines for very long. The pressure to conform? A conspiracy? Probably a bit of both.

Footballers need friends in the media to lobby for them.

Otherwise, you're lonely and forgotten. No one will give
you a write-up saying you played well if you played badly,
but it's a relief if your poor performance is 'forgotten',
passed over in silence. Cologne journalists will always try
to favour any Cologne players in the national side, as a
matter of home-town loyalty. The same goes for the
Munich people, and the influential Hamburg press too.
Look how abusive Uli Stein had to get before *Stern* and
Spiegel criticised him.

It often seems to me that all the bad press I get comes
from Hamburg. The *Welt am Sonntag* systematically takes
every opportunity to have a go at me. Whenever a certain
one-syllable name appears at the end of an article, you can
be sure that the piece will contain a few derogatory
remarks about the game, followed by a torrent of malicious abuse directed against Toni Schumacher. This hostility used to upset me, but I don't give a damn about it any
more.

The *Bild am Sonntag* marks football players from 0 to 6.
It seems to think that readers need guidance in judging
the quality of a game. I play a perfectly ordinary game and
get awarded a 2. Thank you very much. I make a mistake
and the paper immediately punishes me with a 5 or 6. But
I can live with it . . .

The most venomous articles are always penned by
former players. This is no accident: yesterday's star or
time-server is today's expert. The most perverse
comments are those of former coach Max Merkel. His
invective in the otherwise even-handed *Bild* is what the
young players are most fearful of. Words can quickly
reduce a player's self-confidence and growing self-
assurance to nothing. Merkel was once a successful if
sadistic coach with Nuremberg and Munich. The same
style is evident in his writing.

I can't understand why the newspapers should place their columns at the disposal of unemployed coaches and give them a journalistic opening through which to vent their spleen. Merkel is a veteran of the game. He knows how to touch a chord when writing about his hours of glory. But he knows far too little about today's national team and the Bundeslige – his hopelessly old-fashioned advice is really of no use to anybody any more. Least of all to Franz Beckenbauer. Merkel simply ought to get off our backs!

And I wish Willi Schulz, a columnist on the *Welt am Sonntag* would do likewise. For some mysterious reason, he's always looking for a scapegoat to attack, someone whose competence he can call into question, and whom he can insult. Along with Felix Magath and Karl-Heinz Förster, I'm one of his favourite targets. This man is incapable of rational judgement. Instead he conducts smear campaigns, full of destructive rage. It's almost pathological. It just goes to show what an identity crisis can lead to. A former player, never one of the greats despite having played in numerous internationals, he occasionally mistook the bones of his opponents for the ball. Apparently it's in his blood. Even today there are supposed to be groundsmen whose sole occupation is filling in the furrows that Schulz scored in the pitch with the spikes on his boots. Now his aggression is verbal – but he always was an expert on foul play.

I'd like to impress my motto on any intimidated young players: 'What does it matter to the proud oak if a pig rubs up against it?'

Play as well as you can, you young people. Stay with the ball! Don't take any notice of these senile rat-catchers . . .

I wouldn't want to mention Paul Breitner in the same breath as these other scribblers. Paul presides over the rest of them like God the Father, and whistles through the changing rooms like God the Holy Ghost. The articles that emanate from his pen are dull and uninformative, interspersed here and there with some schoolmasterly advice. I completely understand his desire to communicate, but Paul would do better to dip into the box of Davidoff No. 1 that I sent him; a cigar between his teeth would suit him better than a pencil in his hand.

Stern and *Spiegel* are campaigning magazines – basically I like that. They regard it as their special task to expose scandals and raise public outcries. Almost inevitably, they see things as a result in a very hypercritical light, adopting a pessimistic, not to say negative, attitude to the world. Which they're perfectly entitled to do. Long live the freedom of the press! But rather than employing these embittered and frustrated former players (Schuster was reporting on the 1986 World Cup for *Der Stern*), they ought to get journalists to do the job. This is precisely what the editors don't want. They prefer to see pensioned-off players and active footballers aiming poisoned darts at each other. There's sure to be a great row, and libel prosecutions are rarely successful. But do we have to go along with this?

I certainly deserved the bad press I got after the 1982 game in Seville, even though, I repeat, I did not intend to foul Patrick Battiston. In France, people's outrage was then at its height – and losing the game to us didn't help. I can understand why, and appreciate that as far as the French were concerned I had behaved monstrously, But in my own country, in the eyes of my own countrymen?

On our return from Spain the President of the club's senior team was waiting at Cologne Airport to greet the runners-up in the world championship with flowers. How could he welcome back a 'criminal' like me in such a way?

A radio reporter from WDR, with a microphone in his hand, asked in scandalous tones: 'Mr Weiand, how can you still salute a sportsman who has behaved so badly?'

The journalists regarded me as a leper. At the reception in the town hall, the cameras were all focused on me, with flashes going off the whole time.

'A celebration? After what you did . . . ?'

I said nothing, despite all the microphones thrust under my nose. Eventually, the mayor of Cologne got fed up with WDR's harrassment; he asked their reporters and technicians to leave the room. I felt dazed, realizing that there was no point in expecting the press to give me the slightest chance, whatever I might do in future, to show my regret for what had happened. I was powerless against the press, completely at their mercy, victim to all kinds of blackmail.

Werner Johannes Müller, a journalist with the sports magazine *Kicker*, wanted an exclusive interview with me at all costs. I had nothing to say to him, preferring to avoid all risk of provocation or misunderstanding.

'If that's the way you want it,' said the man from *Kicker*, 'then we'll write nothing but negative things about you.'

Was that not a threat? After a somewhat heated discussion, we finally settled our differences.

I had a similarly frank discussion with Dieter Kürten, the head of sport for German TV's Channel 2, ZDF. For months I'd been irritated by one of the reporters on *Sport-Studio* and the way he treated me. One Saturday evening one of the presenters saw fit to comment – maliciously and enviously – both on my performance as a footballer and my annual income – the figures he gave were inaccurate; he had the nerve to quote some magazine or other as the source for these. It made me see red.

When is it ever reported on TV what a government Minister earns, or a Cardinal, or anyone else in the public eye? Why should my income be a subject for discussion? Rüdiger Schmitz thought that we should take legal action against this guy. Despite our annoyance, though, we eventually decided not to pursue the matter, because we would have to employ a lawyer full-time if we were going to follow up all such cases. However, on this occasion I was very upset to hear this frog-faced TV presenter, whom no one could possibly take seriously, talking about my private life. With his fat belly squeezed in behind his desk, he droned on about sport into the microphone. A thin person doesn't necessarily make a good reporter – everyone has the right to be greedy – but a little less flab would be more pleasing to the eye.

As a professional, I'm entitled to expect the journalists who interview me to be professional. Humour or irony at my expense I can tolerate, but systematic carping just makes my blood boil. Some reports are just like the people who compile them, as I once very coldly told a particularly shabbily dressed guy – out of Christian charity, I won't mention his name. Perhaps he'll finally decide to have a wash when he reads this. 'You're a slob,' I calmly told him. 'Your clothes are filthy. Just like you. You've been running round in the same T-shirt for the past week. You stink of sweat and worse . . .'

It's guys like this that lay into us and try to do us down. I also saw in a ZDF studio how one of these self-appointed moralists went about his business in a thoroughly dilettante fashion. He had ten lines that he was supposed to deliver without drawing attention to the fact that he was reading from a script, which he had apparently learned off by heart. He fluffed his lines five times in front of the cameras. And yet they're ready to criticise us at the drop of a hat. I find this unacceptable. I told Dieter Kürten, a real professional among sports reporters, quite candidly:

'Dieter, listen to me. If I put on anything like the same kind of performance in goal as that asinine spluttering presenter of yours, I would have been out of a job a long time ago.'

He couldn't openly agree with me, since he's also very discreet – just as Valérien, Huberty, Zimmermann and Fassbender are. I'm quite capable of making distinctions. I don't regard the press as all bad, without exception. There are, I'm pleased to say, some excellent journalists. The really good people don't need to make sensational remarks about football in order to get into the limelight. They don't need to sharpen their beaks on us, like some of their carrion-vulture colleagues. They shine in the sports world simply by virtue of their competence, their expertise and their ability to write. Whether they're reporting on golf, tennis or athletics, the reader believes every word. They're critical, there's no question about that. But not offensively or gratuitously so. These guys are all right. If I miss a ball, or protest too much, or foul a player, I deserve to be criticised. I've got nothing against criticism of this kind. But when I hear some baldy calling Pierre Littbarski a third-rate player because he misses a ball, then I get very angry. This is why I've refused to appear on *Sport-Studio* for some time.

I much preferred appearing on RTL-Plus, a modest little studio, not much bigger than a living room, with ten times fewer people than at ARD and ZDF. The presenters were relaxed; if they fluffed their lines they were the first to pull themselves up. Their programmes were excellent. Nothing like those presented by the TV personalities on the other two channels, who like appearing on the screen so much that they give a ten-minute talk before making way for two minutes of film. As a television viewer, I want something to watch, otherwise I can just as easily listen to the radio. I want to see action, clips of a game in slow motion, some live interviews and discussions, players and journalists face to face, in fair and direct confrontation. That's my idea of television. Programmes that attack a player in his absence are despicable. Rüdiger Schmitz, Dieter Kürten and I talked a lot about this at the Galinda Mansion. We buried the hatchet and cleared up any ill-feeling between us. This doesn't mean to say that Kürten will now throw his arms round my neck at every opportunity, or that I'll do the same to him. 'Constructive distrust' – that's the best basis for fair dialogue between sportsmen and the press.

16

THE PROSPECT OF
EARLY RETIREMENT

WRITING IS a way of getting to know yourself better, so
people say. Do I know myself better than before? Why
should I have opened my big mouth again? Where will it
get me? I'll attract a lot of criticism, that's for sure.
Nevertheless, I wanted to be completely frank and honest
in expressing my opinions. And perhaps I hoped to escape
a goalkeeper's isolation through this book – the isolation
of that strange player, the eleventh man who stands in
front of the net.

Football being what it is, I shall be young when I retire,
much younger than most people. Only thirty-five. How
will I find a new purpose in life when I become too old, too
soon, for my original career?

'Premature mid-life crisis,' a few clever psychologists
will say.

It is in fact a funny situation to be in: nothing is impossible, but for a long time now I have not been able to do all
that I once could.

Football is just an extension of the school playground.

Every weekend, we footballers enable spectators to return to their childhood. And we run the risk of remaining over-grown children.

I am well provided for, happily married, successful, and I can rely on the best advice. And yet I'm seized with anxiety whenever I confront the idea that there's nothing I'm really good at apart from catching a ball. What do I know about computers or literature, or classical music, or the theatre? Intuitively, on a purely instinctive level, I understand lots of things. But unfortunately, I *know* very little. Of course, I could have given up football at any time. Thrown in the towel. And just counted my money. But just thinking about this depresses me.

Today I'm under pressure to perform well, to satisfy the public. It's stressful to the point of being self-destructive. What will tomorrow bring? Peace and quiet? Boredom? Will I end up breeding rabbits?

Other people have managed to cope with early retirement. And I've got Marlies, so no doubt I'll manage too. But I'm still slightly troubled. What will it be like not to be 'at the top' any more? Is it true, as Arnold Schwarz-negger, the muscle-man from Austria who has conquered America, says: 'When you're on top you can shit on people. When you're no longer on top, they'll walk all over you and trample you into the dust. There's no physical injury as dreadful as the humiliation that fallen idols have to endure. It's no wonder that so many of them resort to drink and drugs.'

Popularity cuts both ways. When you're no longer successful, it becomes nothing but a burden.

I met Lev Yashin one day in Moscow. He wanted to see me.

'You're a good man,' he told me. 'Your place of honour

among the greats, right up there next to Sepp Maier, is already assured – that gives me pleasure.'

My conversation with this one-time supremo sportsman was one of the highlights of my life. Yashin, the goalkeeper of the century, had already been in retirement for many years. He'd had a leg amputated. He could only get about with difficulty – like a burnt-out Formula One racing car without an engine – and I felt inexpressibly sorry for him. And a little afraid: it made me realize how transitory everything is. Even Yashin, the greatest. And I?

I will never go back and join my friends on the terraces at the south end of the Cologne ground, where I used to stand as a boy, but where I no longer feel at home. So where do I belong? What do I know of the way those worthy gentlemen who sit in the posh seats think? Not a lot, and I'm not really interested in any case. Their world is too cold for me.

One thing is certain: my thirst for knowledge is tremendous. There are so many books and films that I have never read or seen. Who knows how many worlds remain to be conquered? Perhaps I'll start learning a foreign language; I shall certainly attempt to master the mysteries of the business world. Perhaps one day I shall be President of FC Cologne – not for the kudos or the laurels it might bring, but for the sake of the job itself, in order to breath new life into the club. It's sometimes easier to bring about revolution from above.

But the first and most immediate of my objectives is, as captain of the German side, to lead my team to victory in the 1988 European Cup. And in the next World Cup series, in 1990. We've a long way to go – so let's get cracking.

The great goalkeeper Yashin was still playing for the

Soviet Union at the age of forty. Tomorrow is another day, and we'll take things as they come. I've never had any problem reconciling my dreams with reality.

17

THE ENGLISH GAME

As I HAVE already said, I was not watching television when the terrible events of the Heysel Stadium took place. As far as I was concerned, Liverpool were favourites to win. I couldn't possibly have imagined that a club I have always admired was going to be robbed of a legitimate victory by some of its fanatical supporters.

Crowds of people milling together, all kinds of objects hailing down, barricades overturning, general panic, and bodies being trampled underfoot . . . I was appalled and disgusted by these scenes of horror when I saw them replayed later on the news, and I learned the outcome of this unleashed hatred and intolerance. I could understand why the match had been allowed to take place, in order to prevent the worst from happening – tens of thousands of spectators rioting in frustration because they'd been deprived of a game they'd paid to see . . . How can a spectacle that's supposed to be first and foremost a celebration of football be allowed to come to this?

It's not easy to apportion blame for a catastrophe of this

nature. The vandals and hooligans and other professional troublemakers, the disciples of violence that our society has produced, are not suddenly going to change, as though by miracle, into quiet sheep as soon as they step inside a stadium. Quite the opposite, we know all too well that sport still serves as a kind of substitute warfare for some people. And the organizers at Heysel are no less responsible, for their culpable stupidity in putting rival supporters in the same part of the stadium. But the infernal relationship that seems to exist between sport and violence deserves a more discriminating and global analysis than this.

To put it plainly, I don't think the English clubs should be singled out for blame. Elsewhere in Europe and in West Germany in particular, we have not succeeded in rooting out from the stadiums the plague of violence. Little has worked: neither an increased police presence, nor the widespread introduction of bodysearches at the turnstiles to relieve potential aggressors of their weapons. A preventative approach to the problem of violence, with better relations between the clubs and their young supporters from humble backgrounds, employing the help of psychologists and educators, would undoubtedly be more effective, both in Great Britain and elsewhere. As the son of poor parents myself, I can't help seeing some connection between what I learn from the press and television about the industrial decline of cities like Manchester and Liverpool, and the outburst of juvenile violence among the supporters of the big clubs in these metropolizes. I have long been aware of the potential for violence among my fans at Cologne, all those adolescents who can't afford anything but the cheapest tickets in the stands. Fortunately, I have always had a strong influence on these groups, and I have often been able to diffuse a threatened riot with a calming gesture. Unemployment among young people, the lack of apprenticeships, a family and social background that's often worse than inadequate – this is the explanation for most of these excesses that regrettably take place all over Europe and particularly in Great Britain, where these problems seem to be most serious. So, in my view, there is no good reason why the English clubs should continue to be treated as scapegoats for a contemporary phenomenon whose causes and effects are the same everywhere. In any case, the first deaths resulting from violence in a football stadium predate the Heysel disaster. Wasn't it in Hamburg, in October 1982, that a fight between supporters claimed a victim? Though it's true that even then the English had already had about eight deaths, between 1979 and 1980.

All the same, it makes no sense to punish clubs for the unacceptable behaviour of their supporters, especially when it affects all the clubs of a country like England. I don't doubt that by allowing their fans to accompany them, Liverpool and other English clubs have often in the past exported some specially British forms of violence to the Continent. But rather than making everyone – players, officials and supporters – stay at home, it would have been better to impose a ban just on the supporters.

The English really have been made scapegoats for the rest of Europe. I also think that banning their clubs from any European competition was done as a matter of convenience, because it is a lot simpler to isolate the inhabitants of an island than, for instance, the citizens of a country with land borders like France, West Germany or Belgium. So I'm in favour of a rapid return of the English clubs into the fold of the European nations. A European Cup without the inclusion of England is seriously diminished. The

Olympic Games without the Americans or the Russians would be equally devalued. And as long as the English are excluded, no winner of the Cup will deserve their title one hundred percent.

As my views on the subject suggest, I am a most fervent admirer of British football. As far back as I can remember, I have always had a high regard for the fighting spirit of English players. A physical commitment to the game, even a certain roughness in contact with one's opponents – these to me are admirable qualities. I much prefer this style of play to that of the pure artists of the Latin countries. It's a matter of temperament! But that doesn't mean I'm blind, and I cannot ignore a certain technical weakness peculiar to English football. A little more imagination and creativity in your game would work wonders and you would become truly unbeatable. Over the years the German style of play has become something of a hybrid. It's still athletic, but players like Rummenigge, Allofs, or Littbarski have brought to German football a new virtuosity, a tactical awareness that it used not to have. Hence, our victories over difficult opponents, such as France. A similar evolution towards greater subtlety of play has not yet occurred in Britain.

All the same, a fixture in England is still a high-risk venture for any German club, and no less so for the national team. I have memories of about ten matches played on English soil that are as terrifying as they are undying.

I know what it is to lose composure in the face of five or six forwards making a concerted attack on my goal. These spirited deployments of players, organized in almost military fashion, are unique to England. Not to mention the regiments of midfield players who go for the ball with unparalleled tenacity.

There's no doubt about it! The English spirit is feared and respected by Bundeslige players. A match against an English club is a test of the first order. Victory against an English team, on English soil, is regarded as sensational.

In the past, if Hamburg or Munich were drawn against an English club in the first round of the European Cup, they knew that their chances of reaching the end of the competition were reduced by 50 percent. And Wembley Stadium is regarded all over Germany as hallowed ground. Winning at Wembley invariably goes down as a great achievement in the annals of German football. And losing at Wembley is no cause for shame. That's why the German defeat in 1966 was generally quite well accepted, because we deserved to lose. I was still very young at the time but I don't have any memory of anti-English feeling as a result of Germany's sub-standard performance. And the Germany victory in 1970 was received just as naturally, because it was quite obviously the right result. But I'm sure it would have been different if this victory had been won on the sacred soil of Wembley.

From my point of view as goalkeeper, any match between a German team and an English team is a paradoxical source of pleasure. English teams have a tendency to play a lot of high balls into the penalty area which is enough to drive the German defenders and goalkeeper crazy. But it's a delight too in so far as I can give of the best of myself in stopping balls that allow me to put on a spectacular performance.

Although they are criticized for their shortcomings in technique and understanding of the game, I believe that clubs like Manchester United and Liverpool, and Everton too, would hold their own at the top of the Bundeslige. As long as they didn't suffer the misfortune of being drawn

against Real Madrid in the first round, these clubs coul
well be playing in the final or semi-finals of the Europea
Cup right now. So I regret the absence of English teams
because I also know that while the English league cham
pionship is one of the most competitive and hard-fought i
Europe, the English game is never anything but straigh
There's nothing below the belt or crooked about it, and it
fairness seems to me exemplary.

As someone who has been classed the second-bes
player in the world after Maradona and who has a reputa
tion for being the 'best goalkeeper' now playing, I woul
be less than gracious if I didn't share some of this glor
with my English counterparts. I consider Clemence, Shi
ton and especially Banks among the very great players i
our fraternity. They belong to the world-class elite. And
see myself as having a great deal in common with them, i
terms of style and temperament. Since I modelled mysel
on my idol Sepp Maier, my predecessor in goal with th
national side, sobriety and effectiveness are what I regar
as the foremost virtues in a keeper. And I find thes
qualities especially in Banks and Shilton. There's n
question of showing off on the goal line, of leaping aroun
to stop 'impossible shots'. You have to sacrifice the acro
batics in favour of keeping a good watch on what's hap
pening and covering the penalty area. It's a great ski
simply guarding one's territory. And one that my Englis
counterparts have mastered.

Apart from the goalkeepers, I am naturally impresse
by the performance and consistency of players like Bryat
Robson, Gary Lineker, Glenn Hoddle and Pete
Beardsley, who are stars in the World and Europea
football firmament. But I hesitate to put them on a pa
with my top stars, Platini and Maradona, who I've ofte
seen appear out of nowhere in front of my net. Unlik

most English players, and equally unlike the German
players, Platini and Maradona possess the amazing
and highly disturbing talent, as far as a keeper is concerned, of being totally unpredictable, especially in their
shots at goal – a sign of creative genius that I see less
evidence of in English football stars, past or present.
I make an exception of Kevin Keegan, who played with
Hamburg for several years. Kevin was a fighter and did
not balk at physical contact with his opponents, but he
also had that rare talent for turning up where you least
expected to see him on the pitch. Kevin Keegan so
delighted the German football world that enthusiasm for
his subtle style of play, but also appreciation of his personality and human warmth, extended far beyond the circle
of HSV Hamburg fans. That's why parents, fascinated by
this ambassador for English sport, paid him the supreme
compliment and the years 1977 and '78 saw the sudden
entry of the name 'Kevin' in the hit parade of popular first
names on German birth certificates.

Tony Woodcock was the other English player whose
skills most impressed me. For the simple reason that he
was a team-mate of mine at Cologne. But right from the
first training session it was difficult for him to adapt to the
rhythm and constraints of the Bundeslige. He wasn't used
to the importance given to physical condition and endurance. We cover a lot more ground on German pitches than
you do in England. Though he was capable of quite
brilliant play, Woodcock's games were always being
compared with exceptional players like Allofs or
Littbarski.

In these circumstances the isolation of English football
is all the more regrettable. International competition is
thereby impoverished and English players are left without
any reliable touchstones against which to measure their

capabilities and performance in relation to those of teams elsewhere in the world. This isolation may have very serious consequences for the English clubs. Not having an opportunity to compete against the best leads to stagnation. Training without knowing how to rate your performance is disorienting and can amount to time irretrievably lost, while your potential opponents continue to develop, refining their tactics and cultivating a generation of players who are better all round, because they have both artistry and athleticism.

Nothing could be more upsetting than that English football should have to suffer all these troubles and handicaps on account of some irresponsible fanatics who confuse 'supporting' a club with poisoning it. But it wouldn't do to bury our English friends too soon. There is still the possibility of some wonderful surprises – or unpleasant ones, looking at it from the standpoint of future opponents of English teams.

STAR BOOKS BESTSELLERS

035232077X	**Marilyn Monroe (Poster Book)**	£3.95
0352321350	**Elvis**	£3.95*
0352321881	LARRY ADAMS **Larry Hagman**	£2.50*
035232130X	C. ASHMAN & P. TRESCOTT **Cary Grant**	£2.50
0352321903	LEONORE FLEISCHER **Dolly Parton:** **Here I Come Again**	£2.99*
0352321873	TOM GREEN **Arnold**	£2.50

*TAR Books are obtainable from many booksellers and newsagents. If you
ave any difficulty tick the titles you want and fill in the form below.*

ame _____

ddress _____

_____

nd to: Star Books Cash Sales, P.O. Box 11, Falmouth, Cornwall, TR10
N.

ease send a cheque or postal order to the value of the cover price plus:
K: 55p for the first book, 22p for the second book and 14p for each addi-
nal book ordered to the maximum charge of £1.75.

FPO and EIRE: 55p for the first book, 22p for the second book, 14p per
py for the next 7 books, thereafter 8p per book.

VERSEAS: £1.00 for the first book and 25p per copy for each additional
ok.

*hile every effort is made to keep prices low, it is sometimes necessary to
crease prices at short notice. Star Books reserve the right to show new
ail prices on covers which may differ from those advertised in the text or
sewhere.*

OT FOR SALE IN CANADA

STAR BOOKS BESTSELLERS

0352322306	**A.E. HOTCHNER** **Doris Day: Her Own Story**	£3.50
0352312785	**BRIAN JOHNSTON** **It's a Funny Game**	£2.25
0352398108	**It's Been a Lot of Fun**	£1.95
0352314931	**Chatterboxes**	£2.50
0352319550	**CAROLINE LATHAM** **Priscilla and Elvis**	£2.50*
0352321067	**JOAN RIVERS** **Enter Talking**	£3.95*

*STAR Books are obtainable from many booksellers and newsagents. If y
have any difficulty tick the titles you want and fill in the form below.*

Name _____

Address _____

_____

Send to: Star Books Cash Sales, P.O. Box 11, Falmouth, Cornwall, TR
9EN.

Please send a cheque or postal order to the value of the cover price plu
 UK: 55p for the first book, 22p for the second book and 14p for each add
tional book ordered to the maximum charge of £1.75.

BFPO and EIRE: 55p for the first book, 22p for the second book, 14p p
copy for the next 7 books, thereafter 8p per book.

OVERSEAS: £1.00 for the first book and 25p per copy for each addition
book.

*While every effort is made to keep prices low, it is sometimes necessary
increase prices at short notice. Star Books reserve the right to show ne
retail prices on covers which may differ from those advertised in the text
elsewhere.*

•NOT FOR SALE IN CANADA

STAR BOOKS BESTSELLERS

0352311428	WHITNEY STINE with BETTE DAVIS **Bette Davis: Mother Goddam**	£2.25*
0352309725	BOB THOMAS **Walt Disney**	£2.50*
0352321970	PAMELA TRESCOT **Bob Hope: A Comic Life**	£2.99
0352301635	LIV ULLMANN **Changing**	£2.50*
0352320931	PETER WEST **Fannelled Fool and Muddied Oaf**	£2.95
0352321997	MARIA WHITAKER & M. PALLAS **Maria!**	£2.95

*TAR Books are obtainable from many booksellers and newsagents. If you
ave any difficulty tick the titles you want and fill in the form below.*

Name _____

ddress _____

_____